Inherited Wisdom

INHERITED WISDOM

Drawing on the Lessons of Formerly Enslaved Ancestors to Lift Up Black Youth

Barbara Ella Milton Jr. and
Deborah Brooks Lawrence

Bassim Hamadeh, CEO and Publisher
Amy Smith, Senior Project Editor
Abbey Hastings, Production Editor
Jess Estrella, Senior Graphic Designer
Kylie Bartolome, Licensing Associate
Natalie Piccotti, Director of Marketing
Kassie Graves, Senior Vice President, Editorial
Jamie Giganti, Director of Academic Publishing

Printed in the United States of America.

Excerpts from The Federal Writers' Project, *Slave Narratives: A Folk History of Slavery in the United States*, 1941.

To my biological family—the roots, the tree, and all the leaves (BM)

To all who simply want to learn (DB-L)

Brief Contents

Foreword xiii
Dr. Joy Angela DeGruy
Foreword xvii
Steve Burghardt
Acknowledgments xxi

Chapter 1. Situating the Unyielding Resistance and Resilience of Our Enslaved Forebears 1

Chapter 2. Our Strength Lies Within: Wisdom From the Enslaved Person Narratives for the Individual Domain 17

Chapter 3. Love and Learning Starts at Home: Wisdom From the Enslaved Person Narratives for the Family Domain 45

Chapter 4. I Am Because You Are: Wisdom From the Enslaved Person Narratives for the Black Community Domain 65

Chapter 5. Remove the Stumbling Blocks—I Want to Live and Thrive: Wisdom From the Enslaved Person Narratives for the Dominant Out-Group Domain 91

Chapter 6. The Enduring Pain of Enslavement: "Joy Cometh in the Morning" 107

Appendix 1. Reflections of a Researcher 119
Appendix 2. A Further Note on Methodology and Data Collection 125
Appendix 3. Names of Formerly Enslaved People Whose Wisdom Is Captured in This Book 127
Index 129
Appendix 4. About the Authors 133

Detailed Contents

Foreword xiii
Dr. Joy Angela DeGruy
Foreword xvii
Steve Burghardt
Acknowledgments xxi

Chapter 1. Situating the Unyielding Resistance and Resilience of Our Enslaved Forebears 1
Introduction 1
Background to Resilience: Historical Trauma and the Person's Fight to Overcome 2
Implications for Social Workers 6
Implications for Educators 10
Organization and Themes of the Book 12
References 13

Chapter 2. Our Strength Lies Within: Wisdom From the Enslaved Person Narratives for the Individual Domain 17
Introduction: The Assault on the Black Body and Individual Agency 17
Deborah's Educational Example 18
Barbara's Client Example 19
Forging a Corrective to Erasure: An Enslaved People's Affirmation of Individual Worth 22
Personal Power Defined as the Ability to Act or Produce an Effect 23
Competence Defined as Capable, Qualified, Fit, and the Exercising of Appropriate Judgment and Behaviors Given Social Cues 25
Spirituality Defined as Belief and/or Practice in Religious Institutions or Culturally Based Alternatives, Activity of Faith, or Belief in God or Some Other Deity 29
Passion Defined as an Emotional Expression About Something or Someone and the Regulation of Those Feelings 32
Practice Implications for Social Workers and Educators 34
Internal Connections 35
The Foundation for Practice in Clinical and Educational Settings: Acknowledging Context 37

The Sankofa Guidance for Practitioners and Educators: Working with Black Youth 38
Endnotes 41
References 42

Chapter 3. Love and Learning Starts at Home: Wisdom From the Enslaved Person Narratives for the Family Domain 45

Introduction 45
Protective Factors in the Domain of the Family 47
Care Defined as Assistance in Time of Need, Love, Support, and Appropriate Caretaking 48
Counsel Defined as Instructive, Providing Guidance and Structure to the Rearing of Family Members and Preventing Risky Behaviors 51
Models Defined as Positive Examples for Imitation or Emulation 53
Rituals Defined as Customarily Repeated Actions, Rites, Traditions, or Celebrations 56
Implications for Social Workers and Educators Regarding Familial Connections for Black Americans 58
The Sankofa Guidance for Practitioners and Educators: Working with Families 60
Endnotes 62
References 62

Chapter 4. I Am Because You Are: Wisdom From the Enslaved Person Narratives for the Black Community Domain 65

Introduction 65
The Enslaved Origins of Double Consciousness and Code Switching 67
Protective Factors 68
Mutual Support Defined as Provision of Assistance to Other Enslaved People 68
Opportunity Defined as Chance for Progress, Advancement, or Community Time Together 71
Pride Defined as Awareness and Celebration of Shared Cultural History 75
Norms Defined as Behaviors that Preserve, Protect and Strengthen the Enslaved Community and Its Members 79
Implications for Today: The Binds That Didn't Break 82
Dual Consciousness Lives On: Our Personal Stories 83
And Yet, Hidden Scars Remain 85
The Sankofa Guidance for Practitioners and Educators: Working with the Black Community 85
Endnotes 88
References 89

Chapter 5. Remove the Stumbling Blocks—I Want to Live and Thrive: Wisdom From the Enslaved Person Narratives for the Dominant Out-Group Domain . . . 91

Introduction 91
Protective Factors 92
Goods and Services Defined as Giving Concrete Aid to Enslaved People 92
Benevolence Defined as the Enslaver Displaying Kindness, Charity, Empathy, and Goodwill to Enslaved People 94
Protection Defined as the Enslaver's Role in Protecting the Enslaved Person from Harm 96
Opportunity Defined as a Chance for Advancement, Betterment, or Progress 98
The Sankofa Guidance for Practitioners and Educators: Working with White Allies and Officials 100
Advocacy at the Micro, Meso, and Macro Levels 102
Work to Be Undertaken at the Micro and Meso Levels (Reforms and Activities at the Practice and Program Level) 102
Advocating for Policies, Programs, and Practices That Protect and Ensure the Safety of Black Youth 103
Concluding Comment 104
Endnotes 105
References 105

Chapter 6. The Enduring Pain of Enslavement: "Joy Cometh in the Morning". 107

Introduction 108
Lessons From Our Ancestors Lived and Learned; Hard Truths to Hold—A Courageous Conversation With Our Black Community 109
Hard Truths the White Community Must Confront 113
Implementing the Protective Factors Through Guidance and Direction 114
Implications for Professional Social Workers and Educators 114
For Practice in Clinical and Educational Settings 115
Endnotes 117
References 117

Appendix 1. Reflections of a Researcher 119

Appendix 2. A Further Note on Methodology and Data Collection 125

Appendix 3. Names of Formerly Enslaved People Whose Wisdom Is Captured in This Book 127

Index 129

About the Authors 133

Foreword

Dr. Joy Angela DeGruy

When I was a child, I remember pestering my mother about buying something for me and whining and pouting when I didn't get whatever the thing was that I wanted. I remember my mother responded with the old saying "I used to cry because I had no shoes, until I met a man who had no feet." Those words so many years ago jarred me in such a way that I am still impacted by them today. The mere acknowledgment of the worsened plight of another person helped me to understand at a tender age the nature of struggle, suffering, and triumph in a humble way.

Later in life I began my research into American chattel slavery, which shed a whole new light on how human beings survive through seemingly insurmountable obstacles. In the midst of being stripped of the basic dignities of their humanity, enslaved Africans maintained families and fostered communities. Children were born and reared with healthy and secure attachment in spite of the brutal system of human bondage designed to fracture and destroy their relationships, relationships that are the foundation of African values and culture. The parenting of children was carried out even though adult parents were permanently relegated to the status of adolescents, and within an environment where anyone in the family could be sold away at any given moment. It is against the backdrop of this protracted, brutal system that this book builds a model for how to use the narratives of generations of ancestors to effect positive change and healing in the lives of contemporary African Americans.

Barbara Milton Jr., along with Deborah Brooks-Lawrence, has brought the essence of what sheer "will," manifested through competence, spirituality, and passion, can produce. This powerful book masterfully combines the complex and intimate experiences of enslaved Africans with those experiences of African Americans today. The lives of those of the past and of the present are effectively woven together to help produce a narrative healing balm for present-day African Americans still experiencing the traumas born of centuries of oppression. The strengths and the traumas of generations of enslaved Africans provide practitioners and lay people alike with a greater understanding and appreciation for how to pragmatically help children, youth, and adults navigate their difficult and sometimes hostile circumstances.

Rarely do we look at the lives of enslaved Africans beyond the heartbreaks and tragedies to their profound agency to sustain relationships and build on lived experiences. Their determined and calculated actions serve as a blueprint for how to create practical tools and strategies today, for moving beyond surviving, to healing and thriving at home and within the community and society.

The authors redefine *resilience* to reflect an empowered intentionality for self-efficacy. The carefully woven stories from enslaved person narratives are juxtaposed alongside contemporary social issues facing African American youth. The learnings derived from Milton's rigorous research and Brooks-Lawrence's contemporary findings have combined to produce a plethora of healing gems that they carefully mine from the rich ancestry of a people that have endured the unthinkable, having survived in ways who have not always been pretty yet struggling well enough to emerge with clarity and certitude.

As practitioners we are often called upon to produce the empirical evidence of the effectiveness of the interventions that we use. Some years ago, I was working as a consultant for a community-based organization where I created an evidenced-based model for working with adjudicated African American youth and their families. After the model was developed and implemented, we were asked to present the evaluation of the program and the model to the city council, a major funder of the organization. The goal of the program and model was to move the youth and their families that enter the program in crises along a continuum of stabilization until they reached the goal of thriving.

The program manager presented charts and statistics that captured the number of those served, their progress, and the number of participants who had successfully completed the program (i.e., who were thriving). I was there to close out the presentation as the expert, to shore up the next round of funding, and I was quite clear about my role. Still, I felt out of sorts about this whole show-and-tell that reoccurred year after year, so when I was asked by the council members "So, how do you feel the families that you have served are doing?" there was an extended pause that created considerable anxiety for the program manager, who was giving me a look much like one that a stage manager gives an actor who appears to have forgotten their lines. I hadn't forgotten my lines; I just couldn't bear to say them. Instead, I looked up at the sea of White faces and said, "I would be willing to bet my life that when you say 'family' and I say 'family' we are not talking about the same thing."

The program manager was now looking visibly distressed. I shared a short story about an African American family we had served, describing how they move through the world and what family looks like to them. The council members experienced a sudden insight into the reality of just how differently the world looks from where each of us were sitting. To the relief of the program manager, the city council voted unanimously to refund the program and to change the language in the evaluation to reflect a more culturally accurate definition of "family" and "thriving".

There are things that simply cannot be captured in a pie chart or be fully understood in a statistical summary. Sometimes the most useful data are the stories, and it turns out there are measurable psychological benefits to knowing our history and telling our stories. The authors have shown us with this body of work how the lives of enslaved men, women, and children, who lived through a period unmatched by any other in human history, can provide the healing balm and grace for those of us who are slavery's children. Social workers and practitioners working with today's children can gain much from following the guidelines developed from these hard-won stories of hope, resilience, and triumph.

This same grace is what prompted George Jackson, an enslaved Black man from Ohio, to utilize his intelligence to avoid the temptations of undisciplined minds; therefore, he did not "smoke, chew or drink intoxicating beverages" (Library of Congress, 1936, p. 49).

This was a critically important, life-changing decision for George Jackson as an enslaved man, someone living without freedom or means, choosing not to escape his torment through the use of intoxicating substances. And who among us would blame him, given his plight, if he had chosen inebriation to drown away his sorrows? Yet, how inspiring he is to have chosen the higher road when there was no perceivable light at the end of the tunnel that was his life. He was the "man who had no feet" who chose to walk. Read this work for more wisdom from the George Jacksons of the enslaved past who truly knew how they "shall overcome."

Reference

Library of Congress. (1936). *Born in slavery*: Slave narratives from the Federal Writers' Project, 1936–1938. https://www.loc.gov/resource/mesn.120/?sp=53

Foreword

Steve Burghardt

Recently, journalists have been writing about the despair felt by more and more Americans as they consider the ravages of climate change and the threat to our democratic institutions. Interviewing a cross section of clinical therapists, they found their patients "in a state of alarm," others "filled with depression." For example, "Michael Gerson, a speech writer for Ronald Reagan and George H.W. Bush and a Never Trump conservative, described his spiritual struggle against feelings of political desperation: 'Sustaining this type of *distressed uncertainty for long periods, I can attest, is like putting arsenic in your saltshaker [emphasis added]*'" (Goldberg, 2019, para. 5).

The reasons for such "distressed uncertainty for long periods" are forebodingly real: Whether blazing firestorms in California, devastating hurricanes in Puerto Rico or New Orleans, or images of sheets of Arctic ice falling into the sea, the images are devastating and depressing for what it foretells about the world our children and grandchildren will inherit. Likewise, the rise of authoritarian regimes, the embrace of antidemocratic leadership, and the flouting of basic democratic norms in our political institutions are reasons for genuine fear. And those fears were expressed before the COVID-19 pandemic!

There are good reasons for existential fear of what the future portends—climate catastrophe, global viruses, reemerging authoritarian regimes. Now imagine what it feels like to transmute those fears for the future into the present-day experience of a young Black or Brown boy or girl living with the "distressed uncertainty" caused by walking down the street, every day, in the present, the past, and forecast into the future. How does a young person cope with the existential threat created because they simply are alive? For adults, this awareness understandably translates, as Ta Naheshi Coates (2014) wrote, "Black people love their children with a kind of obsession. You are all we have, and you have come to us endangered" (p. 113).

Alas, as these parents know all too well, love alone cannot protect their children: Those shadowy streets remain, the eyes of shopkeepers remain, the media images of violence and mayhem, decontextualized and bloody, remain. And yet, amazingly, throughout the 19th, 20th, and 21st centuries these parents and generations of parents before them have persevered and then some. They have enveloped their children in the protective factors of religious spirituality, collective support, and the all but hidden codes of adaptation and resilience that signify survival no matter the odds tacked on through the latest variations of White supremacy: state-supported lynchings from 1880 on for 60 more years and mass incarceration from 1980 on and still with us (Brown, 2021). (See also Gibson [2019]. Obviously, lynchings occurred before then. Gibson points out their use as a systematic tool of terror did not begin until around 1880.)

Throughout these years, the assaults of White supremacy, while real and ever present, may have oppressed the Black and Brown communities of America, but they did not break them. Mental health statistics tell a perhaps ironic story: Among adolescents throughout the 20th century, White individuals were twice as likely to commit suicide as their Black counterparts (Alessandrini, 2021). However, trends in the 21st century are alarming: Younger Black children (5–13 years of age) now have double the rate of suicide as their White peers (Abrams, 2020). Likewise, a recent study in the *Journal of Community Health* showed that suicide rates among black girls ages 13–19 nearly doubled from 2001 to 2017. For black boys in the same age group, over the same period, rates rose 60 percent (Alessandrini, 2021).

The reasons for this alarming increase are not surprising: Our global economy and its spread of income inequality, gig economy jobs, and a labor market both more dispersed and atomized have diminished those protective factors of resilience and consistent support that Black and Brown communities provided in earlier times. Also factor in the mass incarceration of the last 30 years—given trends from 1980 onward, 1 in 4 Black youth born in the 21st century can expect to be in jail at some point in their lives (Alexander, 2012)—and it becomes clear that other means must be found so that such protectiveness grows.

The obvious answer is through education: With knowledge and an awareness of history, a context in which to understand the hows and whys of one's life and those around you can take on profound meaning rather than despair. For that to happen, students need the fullness of their history, not a mix of half-truths and evasions that maintain the edifice of White supremacy through an unvarnished enshrinement of White founding fathers who were themselves enslavers, some of them fathering enslaved children, all of them maintaining human bodies as property. Unfortunately, today's schools find scant success in altering the dominant narrative that keeps people of color in the background, either as silent supplicants or beaten down and oppressed solely as victims. The data reveal how few students understand the hard history of slavery: "Only 8 percent of high school seniors ... can identify slavery as the central cause of the Civil War; two-thirds (68 percent) don't know that it took a constitutional amendment to formally end slavery; fewer than 1 in 4 students (22 percent) can correctly identify how provisions in the

Constitution gave advantages to slaveholders" (Hannah-Jones et al., 2021, p. 77). Furthermore, while the same study found that most teachers wanted to teach well about slavery, they found "profound unease in dealing with the subject," and most found their textbooks inadequate—slavery's fundamental integration into the American narrative was lacking (Hannah-Jones et al., 2021, p. 83).

What this means is obvious: if left without an understanding of their present conditions and the history that brought them to where they are, young people necessarily confront far more than Gergen's "distressed uncertainty." Combine that with an historical narrative of slavery that both diminishes its pervasive, inhumane brutality and ignores the extraordinary capacity of slaves to do far more than suffer, and what a young person might be left with is understandable despair and trauma about their own human prospect (DeGruy-Leary, 2005).

It is here that Dr. Barbara Milton's rich mining of the WPA's enslaved person narratives for their methods of survival, community, and capacity while living as enslaved human beings becomes profoundly important. While hardly ignoring oppressive conditions, Milton's work is groundbreaking in its focus on these human beings' strengths, wisdom, and fortitude. Working from a lifetime commitment to underserved Black and Brown youth, she approached her research from a lens of possibility, not despair. She knows all too well what happens if a young person's life is devoid of that possibility, leaving them with a mix of internalized shame rooted in historical trauma and few external markers as to how one can grow into a full and meaningful life. Her brilliant insight was that some of the answers on how to move forward to live as a complete citizen in the world can be found as much within 100 enslaved person narratives—50 men, 50 women—as within the *Federalist Papers*.

As a committed practitioner, Milton undertook this work not just to create another footnote (albeit a significant one) to academic scholarship but to make a difference in the lives of young people and those who worked with them. What follows is a two-part undertaking: the first part identifies and explains the significant domains of resilience and wisdom that allowed these formerly enslaved people to live well into the 20th century. This part gives academic validity and historical heft to her findings and how they resonate for young people today. Working with Dr. Deborah Brooks Lawrence, who also has a lifetime commitment to children, they synthesized Milton's dissertation for applicability for teachers, social workers, and others committed to work with often marginalized youth.

Their purpose is straightforward yet fully aspirational and exciting at this historical moment: to make the words of some of the most oppressed people in American history serve as guides filled with hard-earned wisdom so that young people come to see their lives resonant with hope. As the Brazilian educator Paulo Freire (2000) wrote in *Pedagogy of the Oppressed*, "To name the Word is to transform the world" (p. 19). For Freire, as well as Milton and Brooks Lawrence, that word, forged through struggle, fear, labor, and the dawning chrysalis of rebirth, could only occur from the oppressed themselves, not their oppressors. In doing so, such re-creation frees oppressed and oppressor from their "mutual dehumanization." In these harsh times, that these formerly enslaved people's words help us all on the road to freedom is a powerful, resonant gift. May everyone—young and old, Black, Brown, White, and all other colors in our social rainbow—embrace them.

References

Abrams, Z. (2020). *Sounding the alarm on Black youth suicide*. American Psychological Association. https://www.apa.org/news/apa/2020/black-youth-suicide

Alexander, M. (2012). *The New Jim Crow: Mass incarceration in the age of color blindness*. The New Press.

Alessandrini, K. A. (2021, May 11). Suicide among Black girls is a new crisis hiding in plain sight. *Time*. https://Time.com/6046773/Black-Teenage Suicide/May 11, 2021

Assari, S., Gibbons, F. X., & Simons, R. (2018). Depression among Black youth: Interaction of class and place. *Brain Sciences*, *8*(6), 108. https://doi.org/10.3390/brainsci8060108

Brown, L. (2021, August 7). Lynchings in Mississippi never stopped. *The Washington Post*. https://www.washingtonpost.com/nation/2021/08/08/modern-day-mississippi-lynchings/

Charles, N. (2019, October 8). *Suicide is growing health crisis for African American youth*. NBC News. https://www.nbcnews.com/news/nbcblk/suicide-mental-health-crisis-among-african-american-youth-n1063276

Coates, T. N. (2014). *Between the world and me*. Simon & Schuster.

DeGruy-Leary, J. (2005). *Post traumatic slave syndrome*. Uptone Press.

Freire, P. (2000). *Pedagogy of the oppressed*. Seabury.

Gibson, R. (2019). *The Negro Holocaust: Lynching and race riots in the United States, 1880–1950*. Yale-New Haven Teacher's Institute. http://teachersinstitute.yale.edu/curriculum/units/1979/2/79.02.04.x.html

Goldberg, M. (2019, December 13). Democracy grief is real. *The New York Times*. https://www.nytimes.com/2019/12/13/opinion/sunday/trump-democracy.html

Hannah-Jones, N., Roper, C., Silverman, I., & Silverstein, J. (2021). *The 1619 Project: A new origin story*. One World. https://www.worldcat.org/title/1619-project-a-new-origin-story/oclc/1250436937&referer=brief_results

Nutt, M. E. (2018) Suicide rates for Black children twice that of White children, data shows. *The Washington Post*.

Acknowledgments

I acknowledge with heartfelt gratitude:

The scores of children, teens, and parents I engaged with over the course of my career who helped me become a professional social worker and a better human being.

The Social Work Departments of Seton Hill College, Rutgers; The State University of New Jersey; and The City University of New York for my foundational knowledge and experience.

The National Association of Social Workers, New Jersey Chapter, for giving me opportunities to cultivate leadership skills, receive cutting-edge continuing education, and be in solidarity with other social workers on important issues impacting the profession and beneficiaries of social welfare policy.

My wife, Kay Osborn, for her steadfast love and support, and for enriching my life with her family in the United States and the United Kingdom. With her love, everything is possible.

Joy DeGruy for her inspirational work, for changing the discourse on the transmission of generational trauma to include people in the African diaspora, and for writing the forward to this book.

Patricia Beresford for being the bridge that resulted in meeting Deborah Brooks Lawrence.

Deborah Brooks Lawrence, an amazing storyteller who graced the book and our writing process with humor, heart, and sage wisdom. Thank you for all the sacrifices you made to make this book a reality. It would take more than this lifetime for me to repay you for your generosity, your friendship, and your love.

Steve Burghardt for believing in the research and in me, for mentoring us on the project, for being an example of light in a world so filled with darkness, and for being a man of great words and even greater deeds. You are an exemplar of love, and I am blessed in every way that I remain connected to you.

Barbara Ella Milton Jr.

I am deeply indebted to Barbara Milton Jr. for trusting me to walk alongside her on this most powerful and transformative journey, and for that, I remain eternally grateful. I am thankful to Patricia Beresford, who over a brief conversation over a copy machine suggested to her husband that I might be one who could help Barbara Milton transform her trailblazing research into a book offering universal guidance. It is Patricia's husband, Steve Burghardt, the warrior sentinel, who championed the value in the messaging of this book and whose efforts and advocacy are unmatched, and without whom this book would not have been realized.

I thank my husband Jerry Lawrence, the keeper of my eternal love, for always being my knight in shining armor. I thank our daughter, Samantha, for being our guardian angel and our grandchildren Sydney and Joy for almost always trying to have the patience and waiting until we can play again in full force.

I am paying my gratitude forward to thank all the social work, child welfare, and education practitioners, parents, and guardians who will embrace this work as a viable resource.

I thank all who have come before me in service to the equity of eternal legacy.

Deborah Brooks Lawrence

CHAPTER 1

Situating the Unyielding Resistance and Resilience of Our Enslaved Forebears

Introduction

Black America matters. Black youth matter. Black youth are from a cultural group with generations of lived experience overcoming adversity. They are the progeny of enslaved human beings and have blood rights to the inherited resilience of the past. We also have a connection to Africa and our ancestors that unfortunately has purposely been severed from our people by a sustained assault of White supremacy over centuries. In 2021, "systemic racism" has been at last recognized for the cascading force of its violence permeating our society for over 400 years. The horrifying dots have been connected: from "slave patrols" to stop-and-frisk to mass incarceration; from White enslavers' rape of Black women to laws of miscegenation to continuing cultural tropes of Black women as oversexualized breeders; from enforced illiteracy to Jim Crow segregation to underresourced urban schools. As the chilling yet abstract term of "systemic racism" is made concrete through the actual expression of a people's lived experience, there is the profound awareness that America is at a point of historic reckoning, not modest reform.

Much of this accounting necessarily will take place in political and economic arenas beyond the scope of this book. From hard-fought political campaigns that will replicate the 2020 Georgia Senate races to battles against redlining, fights for a living wage, and access to both wealth creation and corporate boardrooms, such battles must be fought for many years if past injustices are to be truly overcome. This book is not a replacement for such battles but a necessary adjunct to them. We write as two African American women who are the progeny of fierce, independent parents who were well aware of the gifts handed down to them from their ancestors. They bequeathed us identities proud of our Black heritage no matter the assaults of everyday life in late-20th- and early-21st-century America. That said, we also are professionals with a combined 80 years of experience in working with poor and often disenfranchised people of color (Black, Brown, immigrants from around the world) and thus know there is another, necessary corrective needed within our communities as well. People who have been separated from their cultural roots, as too many African American youth are, are a people who can be dominated, subjugated, and exploited due to a rootlessness that traps them in a world without meaning. This book has been written to help connect young people to the horrors of the chattel enslaved past who are thus solely historically traumatized victims and to remind them that they are also descendants of a people who, living under the most dire conditions imaginable, nevertheless had the fortitude, resilience, and intelligence to survive, create families, and develop communities. We want today's young people to know that they stand not only on the shoulders of Martin Luther King Jr. and Ella Baker but also on the bent yet unbroken backs of men and women whose full names may have been lost but whose wisdom has not.

Background to Resilience: Historical Trauma and the Person's Fight to Overcome

Before examining that wisdom and how it can be useful to social workers and educators working with Black youth, there is a need to revisit, albeit briefly, the lasting violence wrought by enslavement that continues into the 21st century. There is a large body of archeological, anthropological, literary, and historical artifacts from which to glean some understanding of life in the "peculiar institution" of chattel slavery (The 1619 Project, 2020).[1] American capitalism and indeed the nation was founded on and flourished by the amoral enterprise of bondage, whether through the evident horror of Mississippi cotton fields or the far less visible yet connected hand of New York insurance companies. As 2020 has made all too clear, the same plantation capitalism exists today, as does the same subjugation, marginalization, and exploitation of Black Americans (Wilkerson, 2020).

Chattel slavery has a long, lingering, and protracted negative effect on people and institutions in North America, but regardless of where the discrimination,

1 The richness as well as the controversy over enslavement and how it continues to permeate American society was captured by the reaction to The 1619 Project, the Pulitzer Prize–winning project of *The New York Times* and its lead author Nicole Hannah-Jones. We are in agreement with the themes and content of her work and invite readers interested in the multiple elements of enslavement in America, from education and economics to culture and coloration, to go to the website (https://pulitzercenter.org/sites/default/files/full_issue_of_the_1619_project.pdf.)

racism, or oppression is located, the impact is the same: significant numbers of Black Americans continue to lag behind European Americans and other immigrant groups in terms of access to wealth creation, income equality, educational opportunity, or mortgage lending (Allen, 2020; Allen-Meares, 1990). Not every Black American in contemporary society today can be called a direct descendant of Southern enslaved persons due to other emigrant patterns; however, significant numbers of African Americans residing throughout the country can trace their ancestry to Southern enslaved human beings (DeGruy-Leary, 2005). Upon emancipation, many formerly enslaved people made gains only dreamed of while in bondage, including learning to read and write, reestablishing bonds with blood relatives, participating in civil ceremonies, and gaining political enfranchisement. However, much of what Black Americans have faced since that brief period of post–Civil War possibility, Reconstruction—Jim Crow racism, lynchings through the mid-20th century, redlining in communities, and political disenfranchisement—can be traced to enslavement as the root cause of Black American disadvantage and disparities (DeGruy-Leary, 2005).

At the same time, while many Black Americans personally experienced racial discrimination and racism in the larger community, not all suffered to the same degree from the layers of injury exacted by these residuals of enslavement. Many Black Americans who are exposed to high-risk environments survive as well as thrive emotionally, physically, and psychologically. Researchers have determined that these individuals benefit from an array of protections to shield them from the effects of the race-based adversity. While such efforts at building and maintaining individual and collective agency have been longstanding throughout African American communities, there also has been unyielding pushback from White supremacist forces as well, as seen in the January 6, 2021, attempted insurrection, the cascading number of voter suppression laws instituted, and beyond (Brennan Center, 2021). Scholars in various disciplines have documented the patterns of racial advancements and setbacks that began post Reconstruction and continue well into the 21st century (Putnam & Romney, 2020). For example, Derrick Bell, a legal scholar, noted that the gains of the civil rights era (1956–1971) had stalled by the mid 1970s, and in many cases were being rolled back. He advanced critical race theory (CRT) as an explanation for the phenomenon of Black Americans "gaining then losing" ground in the struggle for racial and civil rights.

There are a few tenets of CRT that are the underpinnings of the theory:

- Racism is ordinary and commonplace.
- Racism advances the cause of the White elite and the White working class; therefore, the largest segment of American society has little incentive to eradicate it.
- Race is a social construction that benefits whoever is in the position to exploit others. (Bell, 1995; Delgado & Stefancic, 2005)

Not unlike the 1619 Project, CRT has provoked a fierce, politically motivated, and often virulent counter-response, especially at the local school board level, arguing that its proponents, among many other issues, are anti-White (Sawchuck, 2021). That said, through a careful reading of Bell's and others' work, we find CRT provides a framework for understanding Black resistance from the standpoint of a racial minority binding individual power to collective power to effect change in the larger dominant culture.

This theory goes on to argue that Black Americans have made their greatest strides not in litigation but from personal and collective resistance and ordinary politics, including street protests, lobbying, and local elections, all of which are interventions that protect the interests of the person and the community. Proponents of this strategy continue to advocate for laws to restore basic economic, civil, and human rights to Black people. They also make clear that the battle to overcome the residuals of chattel enslavement require equivalent efforts in education, health care, and human services—wherever Black Americans and other marginalized people can be found (Bell, 1995; Putnam, & Romney, 2020). Building on this research as well as the activist commitments found within the Movement for Black Lives (M4BL), our book documents key protective factors drawn from the oral histories of formerly enslaved human beings that also can promote Black American resilience when confronted with the pain and suffering of the racism of the 21st century.

According to the National Association of Social Workers (NASW), resilience is a conceptual framework that describes a set or series of person-environment interactions (Evans, 2020). It is a process of human behavior in a social environment where that environment is characterized by elements of risk and adversity. The orientation of social workers to the social environment is fundamental to social work practice and articulated in the seminal theoretical work of Urie Bronfenbrenner and the ecological perspective (Evans, 2020). His theory locates all human beings in nested environments or domains in which the person has transactions that either facilitate or constrain well-being. The nested domains emanate from the individual to the family, to the community, and to broader societal influences and trends. Effective social work practices identify resources available to the individual in all domains and when resources are lacking help create plans to cultivate them. An ecological perspective validates the interconnectedness of a human being to others and to systems and widens the possibility of securing resources to sustain human development (Bronfrenbrenner & Evans, 2000).

Another important factor that compelled the social work profession to engage in resilience work was that these studies on resilience were consistent with the newly emerging practice approaches of the social work profession: the strengths-based perspective (Saleeby, 1996). Resilience is more likely to be evident in cases where strengths are operating in the service of the individual, family, or community. Social scientists for too long have studied individuals, families, and communities that have succumbed to adversity and have been very adept at pinpointing exactly what it was that went wrong. Prior to the 1980s, typical social work assessments and interventions were rooted in gaining greater understanding of pathology and disease processes. The integration of a strengths-based perspective in social worker practice removed the focus of assessment and intervention from deficits to strengths, which presupposes that every client and every client system has at least one strength that could be identified and from which wellness and success could be launched. Another way to characterize strength is something about the person or something about the interaction between a person and their social environment that serves as a protection from adversity. Identifying strengths is akin to identifying protective factors for the individual, family, and community.

Social workers engaged in direct clinical practice, administration, community organizing, and social work research have sought to understand resilience as a way not only to promote the health and success of their current clients but as the foundation of the design of comprehensive prevention for the next generation of people at risk (van Breda, 2018). However, endorsing the theory of resilience for Black youth is not a substitute for the work of eliminating social, economic, and political barriers to equality. Likewise, resilience in education is the manifestation of students' ability to get back up from negative, challenging, and often oppressive conditions and return to an emotional state that allows them to move their learning forward. As Cahill et al. (2011) describe in *Building Resilience in Young People*, "It is also the ability to respond adaptively to difficult circumstances and still thrive" (p. 3). Educators cannot support resilience in the traditional learning schemes that do not allow for contributory education from the students themselves. This can only be achieved through equitable dissemination of learning and school interconnectedness, where students are part of a deliberate, inclusive learning process and not simply noncontributing receptors of information (see Freire, 1970/2000).

Given these needs in both social work and education, there are important lessons about historical resilience from the narratives of formerly enslaved people that can be of service to young people and those who work with them. As we will show in subsequent chapters, people while enslaved developed knowledge, attitudes, and skills that increased their chances of survival during their enslavement. In order for the lives of their progeny to improve and to create change in the 21st century, the process must begin with admitting that racism still exists in America and that it has damaging effects on its intended targets. As 2020 made clear in ways not widely witnessed in over 50 years, Black Americans continue to experience oppression and continue to be vulnerable to its deleterious effects. One significant casualty of racism and oppression that is so critical for many Black youth is all too often the loss of the ability to connect to other human beings for the support that is needed to overcome adversity. As practitioners and researchers, we can take steps to increase the resilience of those Black youth who, lacking identified ways forward and drawn from their own histories as capable of resistance and resilience, succumb far too often to the exposure of trauma and other risks in their homes and community.

Implications for Social Workers

Social workers are uniquely equipped to take on this challenge at the individual, family, and community levels as well as through research. The services of the social worker need to be delivered in culturally responsive, humble, equitable, and sensitive ways. No matter the term one applies, "cultural competence," "cultural humility," "antisettler colonial," and "antiracism work" is about knowledge, values, and skills applied in each and every context where one works and lives, whether social work agency or school setting. Cultural humility and antiracism work does not mean that only Black people can serve Black people, that only Latinos can serve Latinos, or that only gay people can serve gay people. Anticolonial settler practice is about more than ethnic matching of practitioner to client. The orientation to intervention is more dialectical: a person can be White and also be helpful in eradicating racism; or, for the client, one can be in pain and also be resilient.

A culturally aware, antiracist practitioner or teacher will operate from the value of respectfulness of the other. Thus, in partnership with the other, they develop mastery of culturally congruent skills used to overcome obstacles that impede resilience and well-being. Such insight on the dynamics of oppression means that the provider of services or education will incorporate a wider lens through which to frame culturally sensitive assessment and interventions. Through such a lens, the practitioner/educator can deliver their service in a manner that upholds the dignity of the client or student.

At the individual level of practice, empowerment, skill building, hope, and motivation can be powerful tools for meaningful intervention. As a first step, clinicians and teachers working with Black youth can affirm and validate the existence of racism as a debilitating force working against African American resilience. Young people need to know social workers and teachers are aware of the depth of racism in children's lives so that they attend to their own stories as a defining narrative about how racism operates in their lived experience. It is important to talk about the "white elephant in the room." As the social work profession itself states clearly, a hallmark of culturally relevant assessment is to get at "the impact of culture, historical experiences, individual and group oppression, adjustment styles, worldviews and specific cultural customs and practice, definitions and beliefs about the causation of wellness and illness and how care and services should be delivered" (NASW, 2001, para. 3). Those historical experiences need to include those of the formerly enslaved human beings themselves as resistors of racial tyranny, not simply victims.

Knowing the impact of historical and current trauma operating in the lives of the youth sets the stage of reconnecting to the legacy of their ancestors' resilience—and thus to their own. This can be achieved by an approach that increases personal agency and power, strengthens internal locus of control, challenges negative thinking, and affirms their value as human beings—just as their enslaved ancestors did long ago.

As we have learned throughout our long careers, once the oral history of a young person unfolds, practitioners need to be prepared for the expression of painful emotions: sadness, shame, loss, grief, and anger. Social workers and teachers will need to assist the youth with processing emotions in culturally relevant, self-determining ways, providing remembrance and healing rituals that are cocreated between a young person and adult. Very much like the once-enslaved human beings in this book, this narrative work can help to begin a process of coping with emotions to heal and recover.

Likewise, hope and inspiration are critical tools for young people to possess. Taking such possession can be accomplished through affirmations, chants, music, readings, and prayers; some of them, as will be seen, are practices first drawn from enslaved human beings themselves.

Building on this opening, the next step will be to identify a course of action toward increasing resilience that includes elements in the home, community, and societal levels. This approach is guided by a framework that places the highest value on the relationship between people and within one's self (Cherry, 2020). Through this process, the practitioner can focus efforts on helping build social skills with family, peers, and community members. Practitioners need to be mindful that the relationship they build with the youth is a model for other types of relationships that can be built outside the clinical setting or classroom. Other types of skills deficits may also exist, and the focus of interventions are to seek resources across all domains that can help to build competence in the targeted areas. Locating examples drawn from all Black Americans' history is a necessary corrective to the singular focus on White heroes and heroines, from George Washington and his cherry tree, Betsy Ross's sewing the first flag, Teddy Roosevelt's Rough Riders, to brave yet doomed pilot Amelia Earhart, or the delimited emphasis on Black icons such as Martin Luther King Jr. or Rosa Parks.

We believe that the outcome of interventions grounded in African Americans' complete history will invigorate youth with hope, help them envision a better future, and develop the goals to take them toward it. The interventions at this level are designed with the intention not only of connecting current pain to historical pain but also reconnecting African American youth with the strength of their ancestors. First, using the enslaved person narratives as a foundation to such interventions, the next four chapters will include "Sankofa guidelines" that spell out how social workers and teachers can develop this healing work. Based on an ancient proverb of Ghana, *Sankofa* means "go back to the past and bring forward what is useful" (Sankofa Organization, 2020). This book attempts to do just that.

For example, the approach at the level of family practice is about empowerment and skill building through individual and familial problem solving. Parents and caregivers need support and training on how to provide care, counsel, modeling, as well as some meaningful rituals. The wisdom from the narratives is that the Black family has always been under assault, yet frequently these families' empowering adaptations and adjustments were made by widening the circle of family members. In this way the good of all family members—blood or kin—can be served (Stack, 1983). The truth is that sometimes our clients are part of families that do not have the ability to provide the full measure of what is needed to support and develop their children. Many of the parents of the teenagers we see are young themselves and have unresolved needs of their own that interfere with their ability to parent effectively. Dialectically speaking, they are doing the best they can, and they need to change some things about the way they parent. Some families are troubled, and some home environments are toxic. What better examples to draw on for healthy adaptation than formerly enslaved people who managed to keep their families together under the most toxic environment imaginable?

The aim of this kind of family intervention is to identify the "elder" or "elders" in the family system (as defined by the youth) who can provide the best supports and counseling to the youth while the adults (parents, relatives, neighborly kin) participate in their own self-improvement activity. As occurred during enslavement, these individuals can be given proxy to stand in for parents in arenas where their child needs support. This is especially important for schools and other community agencies, as communications between larger systems and individual caregivers is important in establishing trust between all parties for services to be delivered and relationships strengthened.

Both practitioners and teachers can assist with the building of concrete skills that can help to relieve some stress in the home environment around effective communication, conflict resolution, time management, and other interpersonal skills related to the effective problem solving people must participate in as they negotiate how to adapt and thrive in whatever environment they live and work. From the standpoint of cultural axiology (Valeev & Kindrat, 2015), it is important to frame practice objectives from a member-member vantage point—in short, as partners. As occurred within homes of enslaved people over 200 years ago, this approach includes assisting parents and other kin with the implementation of new rituals to support the growth and maturity of the children in the home.

Additionally, the practitioner and educator can help to increase the skill of parents to advocate for resources in the larger environment that can help relieve some of the stress related to poverty. When working with family systems, other professional resources may need to be activated through formal and informal referral systems: clinical programs, drug treatment programs, medical clinics, training centers. As we learned from the enslaved peoples' narratives, the wider the base of supports combined with the skill building of the parents, the better the chances that youth will gain the benefits of the protective factors from the family domain.

The implication for practice at the community level consists of remedying longstanding structural problems in the African American community—wealth disparities wrought by redlining as well as no access to other loans and inadequate educational revenues, among other barriers. This goal can be accomplished only by social workers and teachers educating, agitating, and organizing for change with others in labor unions, social movement groups like Black Lives Matter, and electoral activism. As we will see in Chapter 5, the lessons from the enslaved person narratives are to rebel and resist in ways large and small in the struggle for social justice and collective well-being. Like those living under enslavement, social workers and teachers can participate in formal and informal mechanisms to achieve social justice on behalf of their clients and students.

Educational practices utilizing lessons from the resilience of enslaved human beings can be an integral part of antiracist teaching. Such lessons can stimulate "ongoing commitment to pedagogical practices that make small inroads into undoing centuries of many forms of structural oppression that have seeped into public institutions" (Keels et al., 2020, p. 7). By centering the voices of those once silenced by the dominant White culture, educators assimilating this type of pedagogical content into their practice encourage the possibility of improved educational experiences so that students begin to recognize that their own voices matter in the classroom as well (Freire, 1970/2000).

Another lesson from the enslaved person narratives (which perhaps will be seen as controversial) is that the struggle for justice at times could be strengthened and accelerated by the unification of members of the in-group[2] that has lacked power (enslaved individuals) with members of the out-group that has preeminent power. An example of this social phenomenon that was recently operating in contemporary society is the election of Barack Obama as the 44th president of the United States of America—the nation's first African American president. There is no doubt that European Americans (the out-group) needed to vote in large numbers for this African American candidate (from the in-group) in order for his presidential bid to be successful. His candidacy epitomized the kind of success that effective community-based social work practice and liberatory education can deliver and the kind of social change that is possible when people unite around a common purpose where all gain from the unified focus. This commonality is universal, including in equitable service delivery in education, a practice that continues to elude many students, most noticeably Black students. For example, educational success has always been a question of resource allocation. As the formerly enslaved Frank Cannon of Arkansas said, "Now and then a book come about and it was hid. Better

2 Given the focus of this inquiry—the lives of formerly enslaved people—we are purposely constructing them as the in-group and the enslavers as the out-group.

not be caught looking at books" (U.S. Department of Health and Human Services, 2001, p. 2). Books, whether hidden or denied, rob anyone of the same opportunity for advancement as those with easy access to them.

Implications for Educators

As the 14th Amendment to the Constitution makes evident, all U.S. citizens have the right to an education. Given often meager resources, when school systems tried to manage their large student populations, they often resorted to a type of categorization that was not intended to mimic segregation but was charged as a system of best allocating resources through tracking systems (e.g., college-bound, business, industrial, etc.; Potter, 2018). Given a presumed commitment to equity, such tracking would assume to be spread evenly throughout all tracks and across all communities.

However, the majority of educational environments use public funding. Given the historical forces discussed at the beginning of this chapter, it was inevitable that levied educational dollars were and are levied with enormous variability. For example, when the Americans With Disabilities Act was founded and became law in 1990, it mandated the transition of both school facilities and educational resource accommodations, enabling students with disabilities to more readily take advantage of general learning schemes. This also included support for the practice of segmenting students according to ability.

Unfortunately, Meckler (2019) reports that "overwhelmingly white school districts received $23 billion more than predominantly nonwhite school districts in state and local funding in 2016, despite serving roughly the same number of children" (para. 1). Likewise, states with wealthier communities generate greater per-pupil allowances than poorer communities (McIntire, 2015). Meckler (2019) explains:

> EdBuild examined the nation's 13,000 traditional public school districts and found about 7,600 where more than 75 percent of students were white, and about 1,200 where more than 75 percent of students were not white. The nonwhite districts, which included many large cities, were much larger than the white districts, which included many small rural areas. But the two groups each had about the same number of students—12.8 million children in nonwhite districts and 12.5 million [in white] districts. Nonwhite districts took in about $54 billion in 2016 in local taxes—or about $4,500. White districts, home to higher incomes and less poverty, collected more than $77 billion, or just $7,000 per student. In short, as in Arkansas 170 years ago, some people still have far fewer books. (Meckler, 2019, p. 2)

While recognizing the pervasive injustice seen in this context from nursery to college, all teachers are nevertheless assigned the daunting task of managing widespread human development. They are expected to prepare and guide minds through a process of learning with the understanding that it will be core to self-actualization as well as the pride of effective assimilation into the mainstream. This is not just an isolated ideal; it is the right of the American citizenry as gifted by the 14th Amendment. There is an overriding stated incentive to guarantee education as the promise of a prepared society (Dewey, 1916, 1938). And yet the disparity in resources remains as present today as it was when the Supreme Court ruled in *Brown v. Board of Education* (1954) that "separate but equal" was in fact not a viable representation of equitable distribution of educational resources "and [that] schools attended predominately by people of color are chronically underfunded." This is made manifest by the disproportionate number of Black children in special education, which, as Logsdon (2020) suggests, does not forecast positive academic success.

Integrating such experiences from enslaved individuals' past experiences thus will be important, for the lived educational experience for Black people throughout the country has been disproportionately negative in both treatment by their peers and by the resources offered to support a viable educational journey. "The unfortunate reality is that Black Americans experience subtle and overt discrimination from preschool all the way to college" (O'Neal Cokley, 2016, para. 3). Furthermore, Patrick (2019) points out that there are distinct and clear practices that limit, reduce, or deny resources and access to equitable learning schemes for Black youth. He points to specific data that "Black boys made up 8 percent of public school enrollment, but they were 25 percent of the boys suspended out of school. Black girls were 8 percent of enrollment but 14 percent of the girls suspended out of school" (Patrick, 2019, para. 2). In essence, not unlike their enslaved ancestors beaten by the lash for simply making eye contact with their owners, Black youth are more readily penalized for the same behaviors exhibited by their White counterparts. What is "normal" for the latter is "dangerous" for the former.

As horrific as this data is, educators also are in a position to make significant change through the use of historically resonant stories that buttress these extremely difficult learning environments with skill building and learning. While we are not suggesting that you build the plane while you are flying, we are suggesting that the recognition of and further development of resilience in Black youth, learning from their enslaved ancestors' examples of tenacity and courage and hope, promotes the ideal of equitable learning. It is our modest hope that the strategies presented here will assist in that journey where there is at last a level playing field so that all youth can learn, grow, develop, and take their place as contributing adults.

There is an integrative educational platform for foundational collectivity from which *all* our students can be defined as learning through their strengths and in turn define themselves as realizing their true potential: proud self-actualization. Tavis Smiley (2006) compiled a book of essays titled *The Covenant*, whose contributors are noted leaders and scholars from the African American community. They evoke the same theme that Martin Luther King Jr. evoked in 1963 on the steps of the Lincoln Memorial: Black Americans are due their justice. This means real equality, freedom, and dignity. Interventions in this practice at the meso and macro levels can be aimed at securing health care and affordable housing, improving education, correcting the justice system, reforming community policing, improving political enfranchisement, accessing good jobs, improving environmental justice, and closing the many gaps in the racial divide.

As this book makes clear, we need an all-in approach to save this generation of Black youth. Some have tapped into their resilience, and others are disconnected from it. Each Black child and all children of color have a right to live, survive, thrive, and excel. That can only happen if we provide pathways for healing from the trauma and legacy of chattel enslavement alongside the necessary structural changes. Black youth and their families need to be reconnected to their history and their inherited resilience. Empowered with knowledge and new skills forged from the very worst of times, they will be able to fortify the structures within the Black community that can press for larger scale change. Liberated youth, their families, and communities can organize for political power to win on issues that will improve their lives and their communities (Movement for Black Lives, 2021).

Community practice requires strategies aimed at equality and creating equal playing fields across all segments of society. The outcome of these strategies will be to eliminate extraordinary barriers to healthy human development. There will still be trauma and difficulty borne out of transactions with other human beings. To lift the burden of disadvantage from the backs of Black folks would be tantamount to breathing life-affirming air into their souls. It could mean the difference between flying and soaring, surviving and thriving!

Organization and Themes of the Book

The following chapters reflect Milton's archival research on 100 formerly enslaved men and women (50 each). From this work she identified key "protective factors" under the domains of (a) internal connection (individual domain); (b) familial connection (family domain); (c) in-group connection (the enslaved community); and (d) out-group connection (systemic "owner" communities). From these domains and the protective factors that comprise each domain, sustainable social work practices and educational activities will emerge to inform practitioners and educators on how to better engage with all youth to realize their full potential. The chapters and their key protective factors are as follows:

- Chapter 2: Our Strength Within: Wisdom from the Enslaved Person Narratives for the Individual Domain
- Chapter 3: Love and Learning Starts at Home: Wisdom from the Enslaved Person Narratives for the Family Domain

- Chapter 4: I am Because You Are: Wisdom from the Enslaved Person Narratives for the Black Community Domain
- Chapter 5: Remove the Stumbling Blocks—I Want to Live and Thrive: Wisdom from the Enslaved Person Narratives for the Dominant Domain
- Chapter 6: The Enduring Pain of Enslavement: "Joy Cometh in the Morning"

Chapters 2–5 will begin with the protective lessons drawn from the enslaved person narratives within each domain (individual, family, etc.). Their lessons, experiences, and nuggets of hard-earned wisdom then serve as a springboard to examples drawn from the two authors' experiences as social workers and educators that echo and build on these narratives. Such case studies give meaning to the phrase "standing on the shoulders of our ancestors" that is invoked so often in our Black and other communities of color, now applied directly to our work with young people. Each of these chapters ends with Sankofa guidelines as we use our ancestors' lessons from the past to create concrete ways to build a powerful and resonant way forward for our young children seeking the brighter future that they deserve.

Chapter 6 is a summing up from us both where we distill the hard lessons learned and the needed steps, some of them painful, to turn hopes into possibilities and then into reality. Just as this work brings to light voices too often overlooked, we must confront hard choices that must be made for all young people to thrive in the 21st century and beyond.

A special note: As we arrive at Chapters 4 and 5 on community, we have consciously begun to weave in elements of our own stories as a way to express how the lessons of the past, including those with success and sorrow, reveal how connected we all are to those who came before. In this way, we seek to further build bridges across multiple generations so that those who come after us have even more reasons for hope and possibility. May they take from our past what is useful—as so much of those lessons are what we have taken from others. In this Sankofa-guided way, what others may interpret as chains are instead links of iron forged from adversity and opportunity that make us all stronger.

References

Allen, J. (2020, June 11). *Systemic racism and America today*. The Brookings Institute. https://www.brookings.edu/blog/how-we-rise/2020/06/11/systemic-racism-and-america-today/

Allen-Meares, P. (1990). Educating Black youths: The unfulfilled promise of equality. *Social Work*, 283–286.

Bell, D. (1995). *Who's afraid of critical race theory?* David C. Baum Memorial Lecture on Civil Liberties and Civil Rights, University of Illinois School of Law. https://lawdawghall.blogspot.com/2012/03/derrick-bell-whos-afraid-of-critical.html

Brennan Center. (2021, October). *Voting laws roundup: October 2021*. https://www.brennancenter.org/our-work/research-reports/voting-laws-roundup-october-2021

Bronfenbrenner, U., & Evans, G. W. (2000). Developmental science in the 21st century: Emerging questions, theoretical models, research designs and empirical findings. *Social Development, 9*(1), 115–125.

Cahill, H., Beadle, S., Farrlly, A., Forester, R., & Peters, K. (2011). *Building resilience in children and young people: A literature review for the Department of Education and Early Childhood Development (DEECD).* Education.vic.gov.au/Documents/About department/resiliencelitreview.pdf

Cherry, K. (2020, July 22). *Self-efficacy and why believing in yourself matters.* VeryWellMind. https://www.verywellmind.com/what-is-self-efficacy-2795954

DeGruy-Leary, J. (2005). *Post-traumatic slave syndrome: America's legacy of enduring injury and healing.* Uptone Press.

Delgado, R., & Stefancic, J. (2005, December 5). *The role of critical race theory in understanding race, crime and justice issues.* Paper presented at the inauguration of the Race Center at John Jay College of Criminal Justice of the City University of New York, New York, NY. http://www.jjay.cuny.edu/centersinstitutes/racecrimejustice/publishedpaper.pdf

Dewey, J. (1916). *Democracy in education.* The Free Press.

Dewey, J. (1938). *Experience and education.* The Free Press.

Evans, R. (2020, November 9). *Bronfenbrenner's ecological systems theory explained.* Simple Psychology. https://www.simplypsychology.org/Bronfenbrenner.html

Felton, E. (2017). *Special education's hidden racial gap.* The Hechinger Report. https://hechingerreporty.org/special-educations-hidden-racial-gap/

Freire, P. (2000). *Pedagogy of the oppressed* (30th anniv. ed.). Bloomsbury. (Original work published 1970).

Keels, Hinton, Tackie (2020, September). *Ongoing police violence is devastating to the mental health of Black children and youth.* Trauma Response Educator.

Logsdon, A. (2020). *Disproportionality of race in special ed programs.* VeryWellFamily. https//www.verywellfamily.com/disproportionality-in-special-education-programs-2162684

McIntire, M. E. (2015). *The real reason disparities exist in education funding.* Governing the Future of States and Localities. https://www.governing.com/archive/gov-Education-funding.lawsuits-kansas.htm

Meckler, L. (2019, February 26). Report finds $23 billion racial funding gap for schools. *The Washington Post.* https://www.washingtonpost.com/local/education/report-finds-23-billion-racial-funding-gap-for-schools/2019/02/25/d562b704-3915-11e9-a06c-3ec8ed509d15_story.html

Movement for Black Lives. (n.d.). *Home page.* https://m4bl.org

National Association of Social Workers. (2001, June 23). *NASW standards for cultural competence in social work practice.* http://www.n4a.org/datoolkit/NASW%20Standards%20II.htm

O'Neal Cokley, K. (2016). *What it means to be Black in the American educational system.* The Conversation. https://theconversation.com/what-it-means-to-be-black-in-the-American—educational-system-63576

Patrick, K. (2019). *For Black children, attending schools is an act of racial justice.* The Education Trust. https://edtrust.org/the-equity-line/for-black-children-attending-school-is-an-act-of-racial-justice/

Potter, H. (2018). *Integrating classrooms and reducing academic tracking.* The Century Foundation. https://tcf.org/content/report/integrating-classrooms-reducing-academic-tracking-strategies-school-leaders-educators/?agreed=1

Putnam, R., & Romney, G. S. (2020). *The upswing: How America came together and how we can do it again.* Simon & Schuster.

Saleebey, D. (1996). The strengths perspective in social work practice: Extensions and cautions. *Social Work, 1,* 296–305.

Sankofa Organization. (2020). *Mission.* https://www.sankofa.org/mission

Sawchick, S. (2021, May). What is critical race theory and why is it under attack? *Education Week*. https://www.edweek.org/leadership/what-is-critical-race-theory-and-why-is-it-under-attack/2021/05

Smiley, T. (2006). *The Covenant with Black America*. Third World Press.

Stack, C. (1983). *All our kin: Strategies for survival in a Black community*. Basic Books.

The 1619 Project. (August 14, 2019). The 1619 Project. *The New York Times*. https://www.nytimes.com/interactive/2019/08/14/magazine/1619-america-slavery.html

U.S. Department of Health and Human Services, Public Health Office, Office of the Surgeon General. (2001). Mental health: Culture, race, and ethnicity—*A supplement to mental health*: A report of the Surgeon General.

Valeev, A., & Kindrat, I. (2015). An axiological approach to the development of students' intercultural competences by foreign language means. *Procedia: Social and Behavioral Sciences*, *191*, 361–365.

van Breda, A. (2018). A critical review of resilience theory and its relevance for social work. *Social Work*, *54*(1). http://www.scielo.org.za/scielo.php?script=sci_arttext&pid=S0037-80542018000100002

Wilkerson, I. (2020). *American chattel enslaved personry: The legacies of color caste in the United States*. Literary Hub. https://lithub.com/isabel-wilkerson-on-the-legacies-of-american-chattel-enslaved personry/

CHAPTER 2

Our Strength Lies Within

Wisdom From the Enslaved Person Narratives for the Individual Domain

It's just like the wind, sadness, and it's just smacking you and smacking you. And trying to go against that wind, you just can't and so you just gave up and you just flow with it. (Ofonedu et al., 2012 p. 5)

Like your heart is just not even beating anymore. (Ofonedu et al., 2012 p. 5)

Like, I feel invisible and rejected and lone and like erase. (Ofonedu et al., 2012 p. 5)

Introduction: The Assault on the Black Body and Individual Agency

These three quotes are from three young African Americans, all identified as clinically depressed, all with the kinds of emotional problems of so many youth—except theirs are compounded by their personal struggles running up against the shoals of American racism and its devastating violence that has sought erasure, time and time again, of its once-enslaved people. Indeed, looked at closely, the statements of these young people suggest an even deeper relationship to American racism confronting Black Americans: the assault on the individual Black body.

One of the most powerful and unresolved dilemmas of American history is the fostering of the necessity of individual agency as the primary engine of the American Dream and the simultaneous need to repress that sense of agency among Black

Americans and other people of color (e.g., Latinx, Native Americans, etc.). As many scholars on American slavery have long noted, White enslavers lived in constant fear of enslaved people rebellions fostered both by the awareness of the enslaved's conditions and their personal belief that the enslaved people were capable of overthrowing those conditions (Aptheker, 1943; Genovese, 1960; Rodrigues, 2007).

One of the most pervasive and long-lasting mechanisms to quell the possibility of revolt was the policing of the individual Black body (Coates, 2015). Whether through the use of "slave patrols" to capture, torture, and kill individuals attempting to escape, the mutilating of bodies through lashings for minor transgressions on the planation, or lynchings for those asserting their rights more directly, the assaults directed at Black bodies were expressly designed to thwart individual ambition. By containing the body, one could expect to contain the spirit as well.

As American history has made clear, such repression of individual and collective agency has a jagged yet ever-present through line from the era of enslavement to today: from "slave patrols" to stop and frisk; from the Jim Crow laws of post-Reconstruction to the passage of voter repression laws in 2021; from the lynchings of the early 20th century to mass incarceration into the 21st (Coates, 2015; Justice, 2019). Each historical example has a structural reinforcement (segregation, disenfranchisement, incarceration) and a simultaneous assault on the emotional well-being of people that also manifests in physical harm to individuals (Brody et al., 2013).

In Chapter 1 we make clear that these structural conditions must be repaired for full equity to be achieved. At the same time, the following chapters will reveal ways in which social workers and educators, alongside young people and their families and communities, can positively disrupt the assault on individual agency that otherwise would further damage their mental and physical well-being. Before turning to the narratives themselves, we each offer examples from our own educational and social work backgrounds that illustrate both the potential for ongoing harm to the bodies and spirits of young people—and their eventual healing.

Deborah's Educational Example

Here is but one example of how the "lived experience" of everyday life can take its toll on the mental and physical well-being of so many young people of color within their schools.

Vincent, a young Black student, lifted his head off his desk. No one in class, including the teacher, noticed the single tear descending down his face. He had once again listened to a passage read aloud by the White teacher that included the derogatory word "nigger," a word for which the offense went through his body so hard he felt it piercing through him and burning holes in his family. He was to understand that for the teacher, the word was simply passed on as a term used at the time the book was written—so no offense should be taken. And yet, when Vincent dropped his head at the mere mention of the word, there was no inquiry about the effect it had on him, not to mention the appropriateness of the word as a slam against Black culture. The word is to be considered fitting because it is used in renowned literature, literature considered seminal works depicting "classic American literature" and loudly applauded by those educational and literary scholars holding the educational gavel who determine what should be read and absorbed in curriculum.

Vincent's distress at the spoken use of the word "nigger" was ignored, and he thus received the message that he should simply "wipe it off as an offense." He reported that it made him feel like he was worth nothing. Not only was he represented in the work as a figure that is less than human but also his emotional state was left to simmer that his deep concern was not important enough to be recognized as a real problem. It literally made him feel sick.

What the teacher did not see was the correlation between the transmittal of a derogatory term and its potential as a harmful microaggression, the result of which was physical distress on the young boy while providing institutionalized support for others to perpetuate the vile term. Students would utter the "N word" as they passed Vincent in the school hallways; they would tag him that way on social media—and why not? The teacher said it, so they could too.

Why didn't Vincent fight back, especially in this day and age when there is to be more collective understanding of the harm of microaggressions? Vincent didn't fight back, because of fear of retaliation, the potential for a bad grade, or, worse, being labeled as behaviorally maladjusted and not fit for inclusive educational settings. These thoughts and fears have eaten away at Vincent's personal identity. He had trouble sleeping and started to become school resistant. He had gone from feeling he was "worth nothing" to being withdrawn and deteriorating emotionally, his stress levels increasing.

Barbara's Client Example

Patricia was in ninth grade when we first encountered one another. I was writing a column for a local newspaper to feature resilient teens as a way to inspire other youth in the community as well as to send a message to stakeholders that there are Black kids who are up to some good in our community. She was mature, a natural leader with a bubbly personality, but was struggling in her classes and in her relationship with her boyfriend, and she had many problems at home.

By all accounts she came from a tough environment: she witnessed violence and was being raised by a single mother who had substance abuse issues and who did not complete junior high school. Furthermore, the mother's male paramours routinely vied for the attention not only of the mother but also of the two daughters in the home. Her mother misappropriated money for food for drugs, alcohol, and cigarettes. Frequently, Patricia chose to not eat so that her younger sister could. There was routine violence in the home, physical altercations between the recent paramour and her mother. Sometimes Patricia would intervene, getting punched by fists intended for her mother. She would call the police in an effort to seek help, and rarely in her urban community would the police arrive. She thought that odd, because the police routinely patrolled the neighborhood. They menacingly leered at her as she walked from her home, across the park, down the avenue to high school. She would often comment in sessions about how the police seemed to be everywhere when you didn't need them or that they were just waiting for something to jump off so they could bust the brothers over their head or plant some dope or guns on them. She had strong opinions about how the world was for Black youth.

In her home, Patricia had no computer, no desk with a chair, no adequate lighting in her bedroom, no place for the few schoolbooks the school gave her—although most textbooks were kept at the school in the classroom. She told me that it was a good thing she didn't have any books to take home because she didn't have a place to sit and read and think like she could in school, my office, the auditorium, or the library.

During her sessions she often wondered why White kids had it better. Why did they have big schools with big parks? Why could the White kids have lunch outside? In her school they were forbidden to go outside of the building to the chicken joint or the bodega to get a sandwich or some cakes and chips. She wondered why White kids had different relationships with the police. She wondered why so many drugs were in her community. She didn't understand why the White kids were given iPads and tablets and had school WiFi but her school didn't offer the same for poor Black kids like her.

Patricia would tell me on many occasions that if she didn't have a dream she would have killed herself a long time ago. She had a plan: dancing would be her ticket to college, and college would be her ticket out of hunger, poverty, and abuse. She thought that eventually she would become a counselor because she was passionate about helping others. Perhaps one day she would become a counselor at a high school herself. She wanted desperately to achieve her goals because she wanted to be an example for her younger sister and to other Black youth coming up behind her. At the same time, Patricia had difficulty with reading and comprehension. She would get very frustrated at being unable to read like some of her peers. It made her feel stupid, and the school did not offer much in the way of remedial help. Somehow she learned that there were other students who got more help but that they were "special," and she didn't want that moniker out of fear it would prevent her from realizing her goals of earning scholarships to the local college to which she had hoped to apply.

She made a suicide attempt in her sophomore year. It was over her boyfriend, over her family situation, and over a certain sense of hopelessness about her future. She was diagnosed as bipolar and given a medication regimen. She said the drugs made her feel like a zombie, and on a few occasions her mother's Medicaid/family care health insurance lapsed and she had to go without the medications she needed. Patricia's daily life was one of struggle, invisibility, and fear.

I offered her therapy services for $10 a session so that she could have access to support. We worked on trauma and used trauma storytelling, music, books, and movies along with lots of guided meditations and breath work for grounding and releasing layers and layers of emotional and physical pain, hurt, and suffering. I connected her to examples of successful Black women, both living and those who had gone on. I learned of her deep, abiding Christian faith and used that asset as a way to cultivate grace, forgiveness, and peace. We worked on medication compliance and medical compliance. We worked at attempting to liberate her thinking and her spirit from the bankrupted sense of self to the bright light of her potential, her beaming smile, and her passionate dreams.

Patricia responded well to therapy that largely consisted of helping her to hold fast to her dreams and to shore up her grit and resilience with resources and support. The regular, sustained appointments became anchors for her week. Being available in the in-between times was critical too. Those tended to be "on the fly," touching base so that she got a dose of unconditional positive regard and maybe even some encouragement and statements of belief in her capacity to act on her own behalf. She wanted someone to believe in her when she couldn't, when she felt like the whole world was organized against her.

I once helped to locate safe shelter after a horrible fight at home left her with the option to either ride the trains all night or roam the unsafe streets. I once intervened with prosecutors who were going to charge her with petty theft of gift cards at a job she had, even though there was no proof, which kept her from getting a juvenile record.

Over time, I taught her how to access more support and how to build relationships with people who could be in positions to help her, including other teachers, members of her church, and coaches. Some of those contacts resulted in jobs, or assistance with tutoring, or gifts of technology. The more these adults saw her commitment to changing her circumstances and working toward her dreams, the more they provided tangible assistance and moral support. In turn, her own attention to her well-being increased, as her grooming improved and overall physical appearance began to glow.

Today, this young woman is a full-time counselor. She has her own apartment on the other side of town, has her own car, and has her sights on continued educational and professional goals. She now provides life-saving mentoring to young girls who are from familiar circumstances and knows how to connect them to the help and services they need. She tells me that she just wants them to know she sees them *because she is them* and that she needs to help them feel hope because that was what connection to me gave her.

Ubuntu is the African principle that says, "I am because we are." My success is bound to your success. My life is inseparable from your life and impervious to time. This principle is the pretext and context for encountering a Black client. I see you. I am you. My wellness is bound to your wellness. My healing can only happen in connection to your healing. As we will see from the enslaved person narratives, this principle was maintained so that individuals, even under the harshest of conditions structurally reinforced to erase their sense of agency, managed to survive and grow resilient.

Forging a Corrective to Erasure: An Enslaved People's Affirmation of Individual Worth

Part of the corrective to such erasure has always been within the Black community itself, even during the era of enslavement. As Rawick (1972) wrote in *From Sundown to Sunup*, enslaved people from their very beginnings on their enslavers' plantations sought to make the African connection take root in American soil, no matter the dehumanizing experience of chattel enslavement:

> From the slave narratives we can see how the Black slave, forced to abandon his African past and its institutions and to adapt himself to being a slave under white masters in a new land, formed an Afro-American heritage with the social forms and social conditions of the new land. Rather than becoming 'de-culturalized,' the enslaved used what they brought with them from Africa to meet the new conditions; they created new social norms and behavior patterns, which syncretized African and New World elements under the particular conditions of slave life in the United States. (Rawick, 1972).

Their past would not be erased; through effort, their present would find meaning.

For young people struggling to find their own way forward against enormous odds, finding within their people's stories examples of how others found ways to affirm their individual selves is an important corrective to those winds of invisibility. This study found results representing the formerly enslaved connections to internal resources and strategies aimed at mitigating risk by connecting to (a) personal power, (b) areas of competence, (c) spirituality, and (d) one's passion.

Indeed, it's important to underscore that the largest number of excerpts from the entire sample were identified in this individual domain. Given the kind of assault on enslaved families and the enslaved community necessary for exploitation (Gutman, 1973), it would follow that perhaps the greatest strength of the enslaved African was the enslaved themselves and the manner in which they harnessed their mind, body, and soul in the struggle for life and dignity.

What follows are narrative excerpts demonstrative of these internal connections within this individual domain that can be drawn on by others for knowledge building, resource replenishment, and a sense of inner capacity that is possible under even the most dire circumstances.

Personal Power Defined as the Ability to Act or Produce an Effect

Black people are not now, nor have we ever been, powerless despite being the targets of historical systems of oppression designed to make us feel powerless. To avoid the brutality of the overseers' whip, enslaved people needed to be creative; for example, take the case of Henry Wright of Georgia: "If any slave failed to pick the required 200 lbs. of cotton every day, he was soundly whipped by the overseer. Sometimes de slaves escaped this whipping by giving illness as an excuse. Another form of strategy adopted by de slaves was to dampen the cotton or conceal stones in the baskets, either of which would make the cotton weigh more."[1] It becomes important to see the creativity in such resistance and not simply passivity.

Rachel Harris of Arkansas faced murderous violence from the Ku Klux Klan. "Yes, Jesus, I seen them Ku Klux, I 'member once we had a big ball, we was cuttin' a dash that night. The Ku Klux come and folks made out they was dead. Some of the folks run they was so scared, but one woman come out and said she knowed everyone of the men. She knowed 'em by their hosses. Next mornin' we went by old FN house and it looked like they was a hundred saddles layin' out in the yard."[2] Finding such courage in the face of death is not simply heroic—it can inspire others confronting violence as well.

Other times enslaved people used less assertive strategies in favor of more creative ways to elude the punishment of the enslaver, as Henry Wright from Georgia illustrates: "Whenever a slave attempted to escape, the hounds were put on his trail. Mr. W was caught and treed by the hounds several times. He later found a way to elude them. This was done by rubbing his feet in the refuse material of the barnyard or the pasture, and then he covered his legs with pine tar. On one occasion he managed to stay away from the plantation for 6 months before he returned of his own accord."[3]

The lack of self-care among young people, weighed down by so many burdens, is understandable, and yet these men and women born in bondage reveal a remarkable capacity for just such attentiveness. Caring for oneself is a recurring comment made by the enslaved people who survived. According to Della Harris from Virginia, "People lived so much longer because they took care of themselves."[4]

Henry Wright from Georgia says he attributes his old age to "sane and careful living."[5] Frank Range from South Carolina says that "he attributes his longevity to the fact that he has never tasted whiskey, never chewed tobacco; never had a fight; toothache and headache are unknown to him; the service of a physician has never been needed; he does not know one playing card from another. He can walk five or more miles with seeming ease; is jovial and humorous."[6]

Others approached ending or diminishing their enslavement through productivity. One man's path to dignity was to buy freedom: "A slave might secure his freedom by running away to the north or by hiring his time out for a number of years. I was able to save enough money with which to purchase myself from my master, said Jennie Kendricks about her grandfather."[7]

Camilla Jackson from Georgia remembers how she managed to earn a little money during enslavement days: "This was done by collecting all the rags she could find and then carrying them to town in an oxcart to sell them."[8]

Annie Young Henson from Maryland remembers when the war was over and her "master" went to the courthouse to set her free. After securing the legal papers, he gave 65 enslaved men and women a choice, to stay or leave. She says, "Some stayed there, others went away. I left and have never been back since!"[9]

The going rate for a formerly enslaved man who was now free was about the same as a man who was in bondage, so the other benefits of food and clothing made a big difference in whether the freed man stayed or left the plantation. Uncle Willis says when his "master" wanted him to sign his papers to work with him after freedom, he declared with a powerful sense of his own agency, "If I is already free, I don't need to sign no paper!"[10]

Reconnecting to Power: 15-Year-Old Donna of Jersey City Meets Delicia Patterson, 92 years, a Formerly Enslaved Person from Missouri, Both Using Their Voices to Save Their Lives

Imagine the authority this 92-year-old enslaved woman from Missouri named Lucinda Patterson possessed while shackled in an auction block—as extreme a violation of a person's humanity as one could imagine: Lucinda Patterson from Missouri was on the auction block and noticed one of the meanest enslavers in the county and asserted the following when he motioned to bid for her: "Old Mister don't you bid for me, 'cause if you do, I would not live on your plantation. I will take a knife and cut my own throat from ear to ear before I would be owned by you."[11] She recollects that after saying such, he stepped back and let someone else bid for her. If a shackled woman treated as property like cattle can find her voice, perhaps Donna can too.

Barbara's Client Example

Donna, a young teen with low self-esteem, was having relationship problems with her boyfriend for months and months. She suspected that he was seeing other girls behind her back and reported that he was often critical of her body and appearance. She reported usually feeling bad in his presence. She was afraid to cut it off out of fear she couldn't handle being alone when all her peers had partners. Donna was consistent in coming to therapy sessions. She rarely missed any appointments, and she followed up on homework assignments. She used cognitive behavior therapy strategies to challenge negative self-talk; identifying positive characteristics about herself increased her positive self-esteem.

Using rehearsal and role-play she increased her ability to say no and to identify and verbally express her needs to others. She gained confidence in standing up for herself and expressing herself. She tapped into the power inside of her and ended a relationship that was clearly bad for her. Weeks later she connected to a new paramour who she described as treating her like a queen.

I introduced Donna to the enslaved person narratives and other bibliotherapy resources with narrators and protagonists who were Black girls who came to understand their value and worth and their inherent power to effect change in their lives even when they couldn't change some of the conditions and realities of their environment. Even though Donna had some difficulty with the syntax/language of the narratives as she read them, she understood the horror of enslavement and conceded that had she lived in those times she would have died trying to stand up for herself.

Competence Defined as Capable, Qualified, Fit, and the Exercising of Appropriate Judgment and Behaviors Given Social Cues

Work was the expectation. Belle Williams from Kansas says to the WPA agent, "Why, honey, I always been a slave. I worked for all the early white families in this here town."[12]

Maggie Black says, "I wuz trained up to be uh nu'se 'oman en I betcha I got chillum more den any 60 year old 'bout heah now dat I nu'se when dey wuz fust come heah. No, oney, ain' got no chillum uv me own. Aw my chillun white lak yuh."[13]

Phoebe Bost from Ohio whose duties were that of a nurse maid, said she " had to hol' the baby all de time she slept," and sometimes she "got so sleepy [her]self [she] had to prop [her] eyes open with pieces of whisks from a broom."[14] She had the experience of a negative consequence when the missus discovered her asleep while the baby was wailing in the middle of the night.

Reverend Squires Jackson from Florida corroborates the extent to which avoiding punishment is possible by demonstrating knowledge of social norms: "His master, a prominent political figure of that time was very kind to his slaves, but would not permit them to read and write. Relating an incident after having learned to read and write, one day as he was reading a newspaper, the master walked upon him unexpectedly and demanded to know what he was doing with the newspaper. He immediately turned the paper upside down and declared, 'Dem con federates done won the war!' The 'master' laughed and walked away without punishing him."[15]

Susan Castle from Georgia says it more plainly, "In slav'ry time if de Niggers had a—behaved and minded dier Marster and Mist'ess dey wouldn't have had sich a hard time."[16] This was the golden rule, and everyone knew it.

Lucy McCullough from Georgia says, "Ah wuz raised tuh be uh maid fer de ladies in de big house. De house servants hold that they is uh step better den de field niggahs. House servants wuz niggah quality folks."[17]

Belle Williams from Kansas remarked on her keen abilities. She says, "I was about fourteen and I never could read or write, but I can count, and I can remember—Lawdy, how I can remember!"[18]

Women even worked machines in the field. During the war, men were recruited as soldiers, leaving the fieldwork to the women. Maria Sutton Clemments from Arkansas recalls, "I was a field hand when the men went into the army, I plowed. I plowed four years I recken, till de surrender."[19]

Even an 8-year-old had the ability to perform tasks on the plantation. Rachal Goings from Missouri recalls that she was a lookout for the Union Army as they blazed through the south: "I must have been about eight years old when de war start. Fust I knowed, one day Masta said to me, child go out to de gate an see if anyone comin. I did this until one day I went to the gate an' dere was men comin down de road."[20]

People held in bondage provide precise details about many of their duties and jobs during enslavement. For example, Willis Williams from Florida, who was a candle-maker recounts, "The moulds were made of wood and were of the correct size, cotton string twisted right from the raw cotton was cut into desired length and placed in the moulds first, then heated tallow was poured in until they were filled, then the tallow was allowed to set and cool and then the were removed and ready for use."[21]

Alexander Scaife from South Carolina says, "When I was a shaver I carried water to de rooms and polished shoes fer all de white folks in de house. Den I set de freshly polished shoes at de door of de bed-room. I get a nickel fer dat and dance fer joy over it!"[22]

James Bolton from Georgia said he "never seed no store brought clothes, the 'oman done all the weavin' in a separate room called the 'loom house. The cloth was dyed with home-made coloring, indigo for blue, red oak bark for brown, green husks offen walnuts for black, and sumacs for red and they'd mix these colors to make other colors."[23]

Jerry Boykins from Texas says, "I want to tell you 'bout how we killed hogs in my day. We digged a deep pit in de groun' and heated big rocks red hot and filled up de pit with water and dropped dem hot rocks in and got de water hot; den we stuck de hogs and rolled 'em in dat pit."[24] Joseph William Carter from Indiana became an expert at barbecue so much so that he became the griller for the federal army.[25]

Rias Body of Georgia declared you can keep pork unspoiled with some special techniques that he used while a runaway in need of good protein for his journey; he says, "Pork though killed in the hottest of July weather will not spoil if it is packed down in shucked corn-on-the-cob."[26]

Occasionally people in bondage were permitted to sell things for money. Claiborne Moss from Arkansas recalls that enslaved people would "sometimes earn five or six dollars by making and selling charcoal."[27]

Ellis Ken Kannon from Tennessee remarked how for the rest of his life, skills learned during enslavement gave him the right attitude and experience to keep himself alive. He says, "I dun all kinds ob odd jobs, waited on tables, pressin' clothes en anyting else dat cum 'long, but sum jobs wuz small pay but hit kep me 'live."[28]

George Jackson of Ohio remarked that he's smart enough to avoid the temptations of undisciplined minds and that is partly the reason he lived so long: "I live a long time because I don't smoke, chew or drink intoxicating beverages."[29]

Barbara's Client Example: "Competence" Comes In Many Forms

Joshua, a 17-year-old male, lived with his single mother and several other siblings. His mother worked many different jobs. Sometimes they wouldn't have enough food to eat. Sometimes the utilities went off. He reported being anxious about the present and his future. He wanted so much to help earn income for his mother and siblings.

Joshua loved video games and spending hours and hours on computers. He was so skilled that he could override the school's security protocols that prohibited searches on prohibited websites, using "backend" technical skills to enter the barred websites anyway. We contracted that he wouldn't override the school computers, nor would he teach other students how to do it. However, many of his teachers saw his competence in this area and would often ask him to troubleshoot PC issues in the classroom. It was much easier than getting "tech" staff to come to the classroom to help, which simply meant long delays in instruction. Joshua understood the mixed messages that were being given by teachers. He enjoyed helping out, and he received accolades from teachers for his helpful nature.

Not unlike formerly enslaved people who pressed clothes in Tennessee or the Arkansas man who made charcoal, we worked to resolve the source of his anxiety by acknowledging his competence in the area of computer programming. We then connected him to an opportunity that matched his skill set. We learned of a tech company looking for apprentices. I assisted the client and his mother with completion of the application. We prepped his résumé and practiced interviewing skills. The client earned one of three slots with the tech company. He was given a paid internship that fetched more money than the occasional shifts at McDonald's he was getting. He moved through the apprenticeship program and began training as a computer programmer and was offered a position with the tech company upon his graduation—a permanent, well-paying job that began with his skills and affirmation of his competence.

With limited options, such competence had first appeared in part as underground. Think of Reverend Squires Jackson, who hid his competence to read and write from his owner. The enslaver, a prominent political figure of that time was very kind to the enslaved people but would not permit them to read and write. Relating an incident after having learned to read and write, one day as he was reading a newspaper, the master walked upon him unexpectedly and demanded to know what he was doing with the newspaper. He immediately turned the paper upside down and declared, "Dem con federates done won the war!"[30] The "master" laughed and walked away without punishing him. Teachers and social workers need to ascertain the competency behind skill sets among young people and not simply prejudge from established, often White standards about how their behavior has been expressed. At the outset, Joshua used his skill set at times for back-door hacking. If one measured competency within a narrow set of predetermined "master" boundaries—including established professional norms of "appropriate" or "inappropriate"—Joshua never would be employed as he is today. As the enslaved person narratives make clear, "competency" can be expressed in small expressions of seemingly modest skill or even resistance. Given the constraints so many young people live under, we expect the same today.

Deborah's Educational Example

Stewart, a young Black male, excelled in sports throughout his middle and high school careers, so much so that he created sporting event opportunities during and after school. He would round up a few of the fellas from school and create teams. He did not worry about the academic side of learning, as he trusted in his family heritage. He was lucky enough to have hailed from a line of educators and folks who cherished learning. There was support and backup ready at the slightest hiccup in his learning and academic pursuits. He wasn't the scholarly type one would presume would be the spawn of a learned family, and yet he was able to understand educational expectations from an early age. This understanding allowed him to pursue mastery with his interest in sports while staying on track with his education. He learned to pace himself; he went after his associate degree in business just to make sure he was in fact ready to move ahead with his bachelor's degree. He was accepted to a 4-year school and continued studying business. He admired his economics professor's acumen and approached him with his post-graduation career aspirations.

Stewart shared with his professor that he would be interested in working in city government in the area of economic development/city planning. His professor was candid in his response and told Stewart that he needn't pursue a career in either of those areas, as he would have a problem keeping up with the people in those jobs and in those fields since those jobs are predominantly taken up by White people. And all of Stewart's understood sense of "if you are educated you too, can benefit from the same opportunities as anyone else" was shattered in a matter of minutes. He did not ever try to pursue a career in city planning, as the thought of not making it never left his mind. He did pursue and obtained a job in city government, albeit removed from city planning.

Do we as educators have the right to summarily decide appropriate career placement, and if so, to whom is that in service? The teacher's response was little different than the slaveowner who laughed at the idea that Reverend Squires Jackson could read a newspaper. Underestimating a young person's capacity to think, learn, and have ambition is a damaging cultural trope that took root under the era of enslavement and lives on with such harmful "advice."

Like Joshua and the Reverend Squares Jackson, Stewart kept his ability and skill set a guarded secret that restricted his growth and career development. Had the judgment of his professor not restrained and redirected him to career pursuits less contributory, he may have realized his true assimilation into the mainstream and been more of a benefit to his community. Instead, his demonstrated competency and skill set were denied continued development from the one he felt bound by—a trusted advisor.

Spirituality Defined as Belief and/or Practice in Religious Institutions or Culturally Based Alternatives, Activity of Faith, or Belief in God or Some Other Deity

"The master sometimes allowed slaves to go their church provided they sat in the back benches, says Rosaline Rogers of Indiana." [31] Jane Sutton from Mississippi says, "I 'members when I joined de church and de white folks preacher baptized us in de creek."[32]

Della Harris from Virginia remembers the first time she went in a church and looked all around: "I thought dat I was in heaven. It wasn't long before I got 'ligeon, and, yes, I jined de church, 15 years old I wuz."[33]

By the eve of the Civil War it was clear that the enslaved community had an extensive religious life of its own, hidden from the eyes of master (Raboteau, 1978). Many formerly enslaved men and women report involvement in spiritual, religious, and pagan activity. Diana Watson from Texas remarks "how far Gawd had brung her,"[34] especially through the horrors of the war.

Jennie Kendricks from Georgia said she "lived to reach such a ripe old age because she has always been obedient and because she has always been a firm believer in God."[35]

An agent reported this observation in his field notes about Camilla Jackson from Georgia: "She is now alone without sister, brother, or child; but even at her old age she is unusually optimistic and continues to enjoy life. She believes in serving God and living a clean honest life. She just has one desire and that is to enter the kingdom of heaven someday."[36] Mary Divine from Missouri says with a heart of gratitude, "I had it mighty hard in dem days, yes I did but den it wasn't hard as some others had it."[37]

Maria Sutton Clemments from Arkansas says, "I trusts in de Lord and try to do right, honey, dat way I lives."[38]

Lucindia Washington from Alabama exclaims incredulously, "Yes my chile, I is got religion. I seed Jesus a hanging f'um de cross. He give his blood so dat us could live. I knows I is goin' to hebben."[39]

"De hymn book wha' to fence de human family in," says Washington Dozier from South Carolina.[40]

Marion Johnson from Arkansas believed in superstitions: "Since this rain we had lately my rheumatism been botherin me some. I is gone to cutting my fingernails on Wednesday now so's I'll have health."[41]

Still another from Arkansas, Anthony Taylor, says, "I don't belong to a church. I oughter but I don't. Then again, I figure that a man can be just as good out of it and he can in it."[42]

Bernice Bowden from the same state puts her faith in something other than God. She says, "In slavery times you used to carry a rabbit foot in your pocket to keep old massa from whipping you."[43]

Luncindia Washington of Alabama says, "I sho does believe in ghosties. We's got one good spirit an' one bad un. Always give a gos' de right hand' side of de road, white folks, an' de won't bother you."[44]

Whether it was a formal religion or a cultural pagan practice, many formerly enslaved men and women sought strength from something larger than themselves. According to Delia Garlic from Alabama, "trustin' was de only hope of de pore black critters in dem days. Us jest prayed for strength to endure it to de end. We didn't 'spect nothin' but to stay in bondage 'till we died."[45]

Bill Heard from Georgia says, "Just trust in de Good Lord; he will take keer of you."[46]

When a WPA agent asked what attributed to his long, healthy life, another Georgian, Uncle Willis, says, "I tell you ... 'zactly what I believe, I bin tryin' to serve God ever since I come to be a man of family. ... I live by precept of de word. ... I ain't able to go to church, but I still keep serving God."[47]

Using spiritual uplift as a vehicle for healing the physical trauma of abuse and bondage, April, described in the next section, channels the strength of ancestors like Dianah when she calls on God for help.

Barbara's Client Example

April, 14 years old, was jumped after school by several peers, including a former friend who attended her church. While she wasn't badly physically injured, as the fight was quickly stopped by security, April experienced feelings of anger, rage, and fear when in the presence of the perpetrators once they completed their school suspensions. She thus volunteered for counseling.

When discussing her strengths and resources she indicated that she was a praise dancer and involved in the youth ministry at a local Baptist church. She spoke highly of the youth minister at her church. She indicated a desire to forgive and not harbor hate in her heart for the peers who attacked her. Her openness spoke to the qualities found in Dianah Watson, who was 102 years old and in Texas when interviewed by the WPA. She frequently talked of times she witnessed the overseer's whipping the enslaved people who worked in the field. She spoke of hardship and endorsed the old African American adage of the Balm of Gilead: connection to God and spirit soothed the soul that surely ached from the scourge of enslavement and hard work. She said, “If niggers of these days done see what I seed in slavery time they’d pray and thank they Gawd everyday.”[48] She says that’s how she survived. Almost 100 years later, April also believed that she was acting in the image of her personal savior, Jesus Christ, when she prayed for help to quell the hatred she was feeling toward her peer. She asked me to set up sessions with one of the perpetrators because she wanted to “peace up.” I asked her if it were better for her to set up sessions with her youth minister given they both belong to the church and that perhaps he could mediate the truce with the two of them.

She reported to me several weeks later that together in those sessions each had the opportunity to express their feelings and got to the issue of miscommunication about a male peer. The youth minister helped them increase their respect for one another. She said they prayed and read the Bible and sang together with the youth choir. Like Ms. Watson from generations before, April said the youth minister helped them see that the anger would block God’s love in their hearts. She was happy that their faith and belief in the power of God’s love helped them to remain friends and to promise to use words and the youth minister if they had other disputes. Months later both teens were featured in a Sunday service doing praise dancing, and I was invited to attend. Each of their mothers attended, and judging from observation it was clear that warm relations between them all had been established, which allowed April to concentrate more consistently on her education.

Deborah’s Educational Example

My work with David did not begin so much with an active intervention but through the spiritual act of bearing witness to the terrible trauma he had experienced. As a young boy, David had witnessed his father murdering his mother. The resulting trauma had so deadened him emotionally that he was struggling to find any educational purpose at all. If he was to endure as Delia Wright had while enslaved, he would need to find a way forward. Given his understandably deadened affect, I decided that rather than talk about his past and present life, he would gain more from educational activities.

I arranged for a number of extensive referrals and visits, where he didn’t simply passively receive information but interacted with others in the give-and-take of what they were doing. In this way, a circle of trust with others involved in the larger world began to emerge. When possible, I would join him on the visits. I had noticed his innate ability and interest in math and numbers, so one trip was to the Museum of Finance. David became excited by what he saw with Wall Street traders and the work of banks and other financial institutions. This led him to work with me on the development of his own financial plan so that he could attend college.

From bearing witness to trauma to the fostering of individual agency through a financial plan, David went on to college and managed to matriculate in just 4 years. As he did, he added to his own plan a powerful personal and familial connection:

He petitioned and successfully was able to foster his much younger brother and become his legal guardian!

Passion Defined as an Emotional Expression About Something or Someone and the Regulation of Those Feelings

Connections to one's passion were a dual-edged sword for enslaved people; many times *restraining* passion was paramount. All had the desire to be free; many acted on this deep desire and successfully rode the Underground Railroad to freedom in the North. Some passions were so inflamed that death was an acceptable alternative to bondage. As we move into the mid-19th century, particularly on the eve of the Civil War, the enslaved people and their "owners" were locked into a series of formal and informal social agreements, many mimicking contemporary labor–employee practices of the 21st century (Follet, 2005).

James Goings from Missouri explained his mother's discontent with the hard work of the enslaved person's life and its daily degradations by the missus in the big house. "She wuz alwys mad and had a mean look in her eye. When she put her Indian up de white folks let her alone. She usta run off to de woods til she git over it."[49]

The alternative emotional coping response, to lose emotional control with "Master" or "Missus," could result in physical violence, being sold, and being separated from family or other untoward events. Martin Jackson of Texas put it another way when contemplating running away from the plantation: "No use running from bad to worse, hunting better."[50]

Survival meant making choices grounded in the reality of the day and taking whatever opportunities for healthy self-soothing that could be done; for example, James Bolton from Georgia relayed that "sometimes we 'ud sing effen we felt sad and low down, but soon as we could, we 'ud go off whar we could go to sleep and forgit all 'bout trouble!"[51]

Many of them spoke to capacities of forgiveness and emotional constraint that each the AME Church families in Charleston, South Carolina, displayed when responding to the hateful murder of nine loved ones in 2015. Bernice Bowden from Arkansas expresses the importance of letting go of resentment and bitterness: "Now I don't feel bitter against people. Ain't no use to hold malice gainst nobody—got to have a good heart."[52]

At the same time, some people in bondage wanted desperately to fight in the war to help earn their freedom. Bob Jones, 83 years old and from Warren County, North Carolina, lived on the Rudd Planation. He said, "My Marster wus one of de fust ter go ter de war an' I wanted to go wid him but bein' only fourteen dey 'cided ter sen' an older slave boy instead. I hated dat, 'case I shorely wanted ter go."[53]

Joseph William Carter of Indiana exclaims, "My politics is my love for my country!"[54] He also says, "I was always a lover of horses."[55] In his story he waxes poetical about the beautiful creatures that were under his care on the plantation, so much so that in freedom he continued to make a life in the horse industry.

Something similar happened to Samuel Johnson; he says, "On Sundays he would attend church, one day he thought he heard the call of God beseeching him to preach. After the war, he began to preach and was ordained as an elder in 1874."[56]

Barbara's Client Example

Shanique had just enrolled in college and was an exceptional student and student leader. Her mother and father recently separated, and she was relying more and more on alcohol to soothe her anxiety. Her grades began to slip. Her behavior became more erratic, with angry outbursts and conflict with her parents. After doing a genogram, we learned that substance use was not prevalent in her family history. She entered a contract for harm reduction and a short-term course of individual therapy. She demonstrated extreme mood swings and was referred for a psychiatric evaluation and met criteria for bipolar disorder. She refused medications, opting instead to self-medicate with marijuana and alcohol. Also, her parents smoked marijuana routinely and freely in the home where she continued to reside.

She was an avid reader and had a social activist and social justice orientation. She was concerned about the environment, peace, police brutality, and ending racism. She would make attempts at sobriety. She was also struggling with gender identification and sexual orientation. Her parents, while educated and of the middle class, knew little about their daughter's interest in women. The family religious mores created guilt and shame and often sent her into spirals of depression. Often the only anchor she had for clawing her way back up from despair was her passion for social justice and human rights. In her manic episodes she participated in a number of mass movement protests in New York City and other local areas about gentrification, community policing, and gun violence. Then she would disappear when she cycled out of mania into depression, sometimes requiring hospitalization.

My observation was that Shanique used drugs to self-medicate to quell the anger that was the natural result of experiencing parental rejection of her budding sexual orientation and that her experiences of improved health and functioning—the care and well-being of her own body—was in direct relationship to her involvement in mass movement political action aimed at demanding justice for Black people.

Deborah's Educational Example

At the outset, Ken was a 4-year-old with general curiosity, similar to many 4-year-olds as they connect with the world and grasp and build on how to make sense of it all. There was that gleam of wonder and amazement in learning and discovering something new. He had an active imagination that was fueled with intellectual inquisitiveness. He read, colored, painted, and engaged in physical games and activities with great abandonment. His behavior in school was similar to that of his peers and might have been said to be typical of his age group.

At the same time, Ken was often accused of "selective hearing," as he spoke more than he listened. One day he was playing a game with his friends, and he lost. In a fit of anger, he hit a student with a toy. The teacher saw the incident and scolded Ken. The little boy walked away from the teacher, so she approached him and held onto his shoulder. He responded to her hold on his little Black body by pulling away—a not uncommon incident any parent would recognize. However, this teacher then reported Ken to the principal, and Ken was labeled as a risk to staff and students. And, at the age of 4, he was suspended.

This episode marred Ken's educational journey, as there was a distinct difference from then on in his approach to school and learning. He no longer relished in hearing stories, he didn't relish in being able to answer a question or participating in class discussion, and as a result, by fourth grade his teachers described him as having difficulty learning, being unmotivated, and maintaining an unwelcomed attitude. His sense of self-esteem was tarnished. While Ken was able to excel in sports in high school, he never did regain his thirst for learning.

Had Ken's emotional expression been embraced as an allowable passionate expression of feelings in the moment and appropriately redirected, his early love and enjoyment of reading and storytelling may have encouraged his motivation for self-sustaining educational and professional pursuits. Without the support of the protective factor assisting in the maintenance of his academic passions, he was simply set aside as a perfunctory example defining all that is wrong.

Shanique represents a long legacy of Black people in America fighting against colonized oppression. She represents the legacy of Bob Jones, who had the desire to fight against the war but was denied due to age. Her generation has revolutionized America by waking up people to the ongoing scourge of police brutality and racism. America has been lit afire, and for this moment White America seems to empathize with the anger of the Kens and Shaniques in our community. Human beings dare to see injustice and want to change it in our country for the better. They fight the same war Bob Jones and the ancestors fought, for dignity, for worth, for freedom.

Practice Implications for Social Workers and Educators

As the examples make clear, there are obvious similarities among the protective factors in the individual and family domains that can be used to strengthen a young person's resilience and capacity. In the individual domain, internal connections to power, competence, spirituality, and passion relate closely to social competence, problem solving, autonomy, and sense of purpose. They relate to cognitive and emotional coping responses that drive the individual toward behaviors aimed at achieving positive results. As these formerly enslaved people's stories attest, the protective factors in the individual domain are qualities indicative of healthy egos and a developed moral aptitude that enables the holder of these qualities to appraise situations thoroughly and to make a conscious decision about the type of response required to avoid negative consequences. It seems that formerly enslaved men and women in the study endorse the use of religious and spiritual coping processes, similar to what is described in contemporary literature for adolescent African Americans.

It is important to note that while the findings in each chapter will focus on a single protective factor, this in no way suggests that African American youth need have only one strategy in operation at a time in order to fend off adversity. In fact, it is likely that the opposite is more true: multiple protective factors across multiple domains may need to be operating to achieve sufficient protections to promote resilience. Additionally, in the period of adolescence some protective factors may germinate as opposed to being immediately expressed; the process of maturity over time can and will give rise to better developed resilience strategies.

Internal Connections

For professionals working with adolescents, the anecdotes and insights from formerly enslaved ancestors are to be used to help foster conversations on how people, under even the most dire circumstances of truly limited control—never forget, the enslaved people were property, not people—one can still locate within themselves a source of personal power and agency. No matter how limited, a person can develop thoughts and actions related to their ability to overcome. Teens can use their personal power in the service of goals that can carry them to their dreams. Connecting to power means knowing the limits of your own power and knowing when you need more skill development or assistance from someone outside of yourself.

Connecting to competence is a way of directing personal power and energy into efforts aimed at improving a young person's chances for success and achievement. Not everything can be addressed at once. Competence is about understanding what skill set is needed now to get you through to the next level. It's about developing the capacity to accept and acquire instruction and support to fine-tune whatever natural talent one already has. Connecting to competence helps to build confidence in judgment, which can provide important protections when faced with unpredictable or unanticipated situations.

Likewise, as the interviews make clear, a connection to spirituality has deep roots in the African American family. Many adolescents, in their process of individuation and identity formation, are trying to figure out what spirituality means to them, which is separate and distinct from their parents. At this stage it is common to see rebellion, and only parents with the firmest grip on their teens are successful in getting their teens to their houses of worship. This disconnection from a cultural strength places youth at higher risk. As the literature makes clear, those youth who do not detach from their spiritual and religious practices do achieve a modicum of advantage over some of their peers (Utsey et al., 2008). For these teens, houses of worship provide important opportunities for mentoring as well as safe havens of bustling activity for youth. These teens frequently speak of a faith that helps them to believe better days are ahead, and they receive hope for their journey. Professionals need to overcome their fears of over-reach to address this arena of strength as well.

Furthermore, the narratives help one understand that connecting to passion is a way to connect to joy and other emotions. If a human being treated no differently than cattle can locate such passion, then it is critical work for social workers and teachers to do the same with the young people with whom they work. When the environment offers up little happiness, teens can still locate and connect to their passion, too. They need to be encouraged to do so, whether it is music, sports, movies, or video games. Laughter, movement, imagination, and play are important buffers to trauma and pain.

Finally, in adolescence it is not uncommon to begin to take steps toward career interests. Teens begin to enter the world of work and volunteerism. Not unlike those formerly enslaved ancestors who find purpose and meaning, teens, like David, who develop and possess a future orientation can then begin to combat the despair that may accompany the reality that many adults—not unlike the "slaveowners" of 150 years ago—have lost hope in the promise of the young people around them. Helping them connect to their passion means adults take time to learn about that teen's hobby or interest, reading magazines about it, researching it, reaching out to others for a better understanding of it. For example, paying attention to rap music becomes an opportunity to tap into their pain and their possibility, not judgment.

At the same time, other narratives make clear that passion sometimes needs to be restrained in favor of other priorities in order to survive the moment. "Survival" for enslaved people was a daily strategy, not a once-in-a-lifetime event. As the unfolding murders of so many young Black and Brown men and women at the hands of police make clear in 2020, such strategies remain ever present in our communities—whether a small city in Minnesota or on the streets of Chicago. Our recommendations cannot overcome the conditions and mindsets that allow such horrors to continue at such an unending, unyielding pace. However, not unlike what some of the formerly enslaved men and women make clear, one can help young people consider what could happen if their own reactions escalate too quickly. This is not written to suggest the responsibility for such violence lies with them; it is to do whatever it takes—whether tools, inner self-regulation, or deep breathing—to keep them alive. That's why, even under chattel enslavement, in the face of adversity it was and is important to be levelheaded, calm, and collected so as not to make a horrific situation even worse. This is where competence, power, and spirituality overlap and may be required to be used in tandem to avoid catastrophe. These individual connections were effective protections for our enslaved ancestors and can be a roadmap to resilience in the individual domain.

The Foundation for Practice in Clinical and Educational Settings: Acknowledging Context

At the individual level of practice, empowerment, skill building, hope, and motivation can be powerful tools for intervention (Bandy & Moore, 2013). As a first step, however, clinicians working with African American and Latinx youth must affirm and validate the existence of racism as a debilitating force working against their resilience. Young people need to know social workers know something about racism but that their story will be the definitive story about how racism operates in their lives. It is important to talk about the white elephant in the room. A hallmark of culturally competent assessment is to get at "the impact of culture, historical experiences, individual and group oppression, adjustment styles, worldviews and specific cultural customs and practice, definitions and beliefs about the causation of wellness and illness and how care and services should be delivered" (NASW, 2001, para. 3).

Using the material from these narratives means a practitioner must incorporate a deep understanding of the lived experience of enslavement itself in order to enable young people to locate their own survival strategies as important and powerful. All too often, popular culture and the ever-present search for simple explanations can lead well-meaning people to impose 21st-century assumptions and context onto earlier generations' behavior and attitudes. Read out of context, many of the enslaved person narratives could seem illiterate, extremely modest in both aspiration and achievement—shining a pair of shoes, happy for a nickel, satisfied to have worshiped at a humble church. Woven into the fabric of society that owned you in the same way one owns farm animals, with the same freedom to put them to death at any moment for the most minor of reasons, their small deeds of affirmation become extraordinary acts of brave resistance, not passivity. While living in a world defined by the unending trauma of not being seen as a human being, their words provide hope alongside the heartache (Mental Health America, 2021).

Thus, knowing and openly acknowledging the impact of historical and current trauma operating in the lives of the youth can set the stage of reconnecting to the legacy of their resilience. This can be achieved by an approach that uses the narrative examples to increase personal agency and power, strengthen internal locus of control, challenge negative thinking, and affirm value as human beings. When Vincent and Patricia find the power in the stories of their enslaved ancestors, steps toward finding their own power become a possibility.

This does not mean that exploring these enslaved person narratives will be an easy panacea. As their oral history unfolds, practitioners and teachers need to be prepared for the expression of pain and emotions: sadness, shame, loss, grief, and anger. By weaving elements from the stories that resemble elements of their own, one can assist youth with processing emotions in ways that become culturally relevant and historically rooted. One can allow for remembrance and healing rituals that are cocreated, thus helping to begin coping effectively with their emotions. Asking them to imagine how an enslaved female stood up to Ku Klux Klan members by brilliantly connecting their horses to their owners can help Vincent find within himself the power to question the use of the "n" word by his teacher. Hope and inspiration—not only from famous heroes like Nelson Mandela or Harriet Tubman but also from everyday folks like Bob Jones and Diana Watson—are critical tools for young people to possess.

Over time, this work with the individual domain will utilize the distinct protective factors discussed: (a) connecting to personal power, (b) connecting to areas of competence, (c) connecting to spirituality, and (d) connecting to one's passion.

The Sankofa Guidance for Practitioners and Educators: Working with Black Youth

1. Learn brain science and adolescent brain development. How would you respond to perceived threats if you were in fight-or-flight mode? Our Black children are so overexposed to trauma, grief, and loss that their brains are swimming in cortisol and other hormones. The frontal lobe and frontal cortex of adolescents are not fully formed until well into young adulthood. The cortex is responsible for movement, speech control, expression of emotions, and reasoning, all of which go out the door when in fight-or-flight mode. For adolescents to arise out of bed in the morning to engage in life is Herculean. It speaks to an exceptional desire to live. Using exemplars of the past from the narratives of people who themselves got up out of the roughest of beds and through competency persevered can aid young people as they seek to overcome their own constrained work environments.

2. Mind your microaggressions. Our Black and Brown children awake in the morning, and throughout the day much of their intake of messages about them as precious and sacred human beings is assaulted. The messages come in from the abject neglect of their communities, the experiences of economic struggle, the detachment from essential resources, the cruelty of violence and poverty, and the encounters with authority figures, including parents, who internalize shame and homophobia. By the time they show up in our agencies, offices, and schools, they are wounded.

We therefore must take care not to further the injury and cycle of shame through seemingly small acts of indifference that intensify that trauma (Office of Behavioral Health Equity [OBHE], 2020). For example, for Vincent, it was the use of the "n" word, that single word, ostensibly a simple microaggression, that held the overarching message of "get over it" and not only minimized his experience and worth but, more importantly, denied the strength he realized from his love of writing. By nature, he was too introverted to socialize in the usually accepted clubs or athletic ventures. He found soundness in reading and writing, activities his family shook their collective heads at, as the general familial consensus was that he would not be able to sustain himself by putting words on paper—and yet it was his strength, his fortitude, his identity. He would continue writing, but only in silence and solitude, and the minute he anticipated anyone coming near he would close the book, hiding what he was writing, in much the same way as the enslaved man who turned the newspaper upside down so the "master" would not know he could read.

3. Abandon the concept of tough love. Black and Brown children don't need "toughness"; life is already tough for the overwhelming majority of them. They need an abundance of love that is propped up on empathy and compassion. Practitioners need to recognize this ugly fact and dig deep into understanding their lives and obtain from Black youth the full measure of their narrative. Unlike the White "masters," get to know Black youth, their circumstances, the targeted areas for intervention, and all their strengths. Chances are they lost the capacity to access their sense of knowing their strengths and need guidance, identification, fortification, and affirmation of their strengths. Look underneath behaviors and attitudes that at first blush may seem arrogant and even antisocial but that are likely expressions of ability with no easy outlets for such abilities to shine—just as their enslaved ancestors did.

Understand and embrace their spiritual and religious outlets as supremely important vehicles for strength and healing. It is no accident that there is a deep religious tradition within Black communities. Their enslaved ancestors used its strengths to help them survive with dignity under horribly constrained conditions. With appropriate guidance, young people can lean on such strengths as well.

4. Do not be afraid. If you are afraid of that Black teen, then you have no business entering a therapeutic relationship with that teen. If you do not see that Black child as a fully endowed human being whose behavior is shaped by a confluence of societal and external factors, then you should not enter a therapeutic relationship with that teenager. If you do not believe in the inherent worth and value of that Black teenager, then you should not enter that sacred relationship. And for however long you are blessed to engage with that precious human being, be mindful of the need to inspire hope. Black youth know their worth and experience esteem when they master a skill, demonstrate empathy for others, and participate in the spiritual practices of their ancestors. They are their ancestors manifest; they understand they have to speak up and be willing to risk it all, like Lucinda Patterson. They must embrace that sacred part of them that wants to survive and live life as fully as they are able given the external forces that constantly act against the fundamental truth that all life seeks to survive.

Bring your true self into the relationship. Be humble. Be curious, and do not be afraid to let this Black teenager lead the way in the sessions. They are the authors and owners of their own life story. We can help them change the trajectory of the arc of the story by engaging in human validation and making them visible and helping them identify, grow, and access the resources inside them and around them to improve their lives. It's a partnership.

Black youth's anger is justifiable. Let them have it. Help them channel it. Help them transform it. Walk a day in their shoes. Feel what it is like to be the sustained target of scrutiny and social control. Feel what it is like to know pathways forward are riddled with hurdles and roadblocks and potholes and that as Black youth age the way out becomes more and more narrow and that it has little to do with anything you do. It's infuriating. It's frustrating. It's debilitating. It's traumatizing. Black youth are told from the earliest of ages to not speak up, not speak out, and not speak back to adults, to authority, and to the White man. Black youth reject the muzzling of their thoughts and ideas and emotions, and just like their ancestors they are mindful of the time and place for discharging their righteous anger, and their hopes are always in the direction of freedom from social control and oppression.

5. Allow Black youth to be youth! It is too often the case that the "boys will be boys" moniker only holds for White boys. Black youth are held to a different standard. Tamir Rice was a 12-year-old kid playing in a park, or the closest thing to a park, in a housing development area with a toy gun and was shot dead by the police! Do you really think that if Tamir Rice was White that that would have happened? You know the answer is no.

Black kids need to be kids. They screw up. They make mistakes. They explore. They do stupid things. All kids do this. Black kids are entitled to this rite of passage too and are too often denied it. White people too often see Black youth as grown adults. And parents help with this too. I myself had keys to my home at 9 years old. I was parentified. Many of my male clients were the "men of the house," and that's a dangerous mixed message for a fragile adolescent mind to absorb. Then we wonder why we can't reign in defiant behaviors or sexualized behaviors, but once the horse has left the barn it can be hard to corral it back. Kids need to be able to be kids.

The protective factors of the individual domain relate to cognitive and emotional coping responses that drive the individual toward behaviors aimed at achieving positive results. The protective factors in the individual domain are qualities indicative of healthy egos and a developed moral aptitude that enable the holder of these qualities to appraise situations thoroughly and to make a conscious decision about the type of response required to avoid negative consequences. Practitioners in social work and education are able to achieve progress with youth on the path to goal attainment when resilience is rooted in the personal domain and the change process can be sustained when there is concurrent intervention in the family domain.

As the next chapter elucidates, the way to generalize positive gains in the resilience of Black and Brown youth is to connect to their families. As the enslaved person narratives make clear, enslaved men and women spoke clearly about the importance of the family during bondage. "Master" configured the families, usually without regard for blood ties, as family fragmentation was a critical element of subjugation in the system of enslavement. And despite that, Black men and women coalesced in their quarters and functioned as family with very clear and present dynamics and defined levels of parental engagement and support. They did their best to protect and raise children while they were in their charge. Such lessons inform future efforts with our young people as well.

Endnotes

Excerpts from the Federal Writers' Project Slave Narrative (FWPSN) Collection

1. FWPSN, Georgia, Part 4, p. 195
2. FWPSN, Arkansas, Part 3, p. 180
3. FWPSN, Georgia, Part 4, p. 202
4. FWPSN, Virginia, p. 26
5. FWPSN, Georgia, Part 4, p. 204
6. FWPSN, South Carolina, Part 4, p. 3
7. FWPSN, Georgia, Part 3, p. 6
8. FWPSN, Georgia, Part 2, p. 297
9. FWPSN, Maryland, p. 28
10. FWPSN, Georgia, Part 4, p. 171
11. FWPSN, Missouri, p. 270
12. FWPSN, Kansas, p. 15
13. FWPSN, South Carolina, Part 1, p. 57
14. FWPSN, Ohio, p. 10
15. FWPSN, Florida, p. 178
16. FWPSN, Georgia, Part 1, p. 182
17. FWPSN, Georgia, Part 3, p. 67
18. FWPSN, Kansas, p. 16
19. FWPSN, Arkansas, Part 2, p. 16
20. FWPSN, Missouri, p. 122
21. FWPSN, Florida, p. 349
22. FWPSN, South Carolina, Part 4, p. 76
23. FWPSN, Georgia, Part 1, p. 94
24. FWPSN, Texas, Part 1, p. 123
25. FWPSN, Indiana, p. 48
26. FWPSN, Georgia, Part 1, p. 90
27. FWPSN, Arkansas, Part 5, p. 160

28. FWPSN, Tennessee, p. 39
29. FWPSN, Ohio, p. 49
30. FWPSN, Florida, p. 178
31. FWPSN, Indiana, p. 165
32. FWPSN, Mississippi, p. 152
33. FWPSN, Virginia, p. 24
34. FWPSN, Texas, Part 4, p. 145
35. FWPSN, Georgia, Part 3, p. 6
36. FWPSN, Georgia, Part 2, p. 298
37. FWPSN, Missouri, p. 104
38. FWPSN, Arkansas, Part 2, p. 22
39. FWPSN, Alabama, p. 410
40. FWPSN, South Carolina, Part 1, p. 332
41. FWPSN, Arkansas, Part 4, p. 113
42. FWPSN, Arkansas, Part 6, p. 263
43. FWPSN, Arkansas, Part 3, p. 166
44. FWPSN, Alabama, p. 410
45. FWPSN, Alabama, p. 131
46. FWPSN, Georgia, Part 2, p. 146
47. FWPSN, Georgia, Part 4, p. 174
48. FWPSN, Texas, Part 4, p. 145
49. FWPSN, Missouri, p. 121
50. FWPSN, Texas, Part 2, p. 189
51. FWPSN, Georgia, Part 1, p. 100
52. FWPSN, Arkansas, Part 4, p. 282
53. FWPSN, North Carolina, Part 2, p. 24
54. FWPSN, Indiana, p. 48
55. FWPSN, Indiana, p. 48
56. FWPSN, Florida, p. 189

References

American Psychological Association. (2021). Black and African American communities and mental health. https://www.apa.org/topics/racism-bias-discrimination/health-disparities-stress

Aptheker, H. (1943). *American negro slave revolts*. Columbia University Press. https://doi.org/10.7312/apth90268

Bandy, T., & Moore, K. A. (2013). *What works for African American children and adolescents: Lessons from experimental evaluations of programs and interventions*. Child Trends. http://www.childtrends.org/wp-content/uploads/2013/05/2011-04WhatWorkAAChildren.pdf.

Brody, G. H., Yu, T., Chen, E., Miller, G. E., Kogan, S. M., & Beach, S. R. H. (2013). Is resilience only skin deep? Rural African Americans' socioeconomic status-related risk and competence in preadolescence and psychological adjustment and allostatic load at age 19. *Psychological Science, 24*(7), 1285–1293.

Coates , T. (2015). *Between the world and me*. Spiegel & Grau.

Genovese, E. D. (1961). The slave South: An interpretation. *Science & Society, 25*(4), 320–337. http://www.jstor.org/stable/40400766

Gutman, H. G. (1973). *Readings in American social history*, 1600–1876 (Vol. 1). Prentice Hall.

Follett, R. J. (2005). *The sugar masters: Planters and slaves in Louisiana' s cane world.* LSU Press.

Mental Health America. (2021). *Black and African American communities and mental health.* https://www.mhanational.org/issues/black-and-african-american-communities-and-mental-health.

National Association of Social Workers. (2001, June 23). *NASW standards for cultural competence in social work practice.* http://www.n4a.org/datoolkit/NASW%20Standards%20II.htm

Office of Behavioral Health Equity. (2020). *Trauma, racism, chronic stress, and the health of Black Americans.* https://namivirginia.org/wp-content/uploads/sites/127/2020/06/What-the-Research-says-AfricanAmericansRaceViolenceandHealth-OBHE-6.3.20-pm.pdf

Ofonedu, M. E., Percy, W. H., Harris-Britt, A., & Belcher, H. M. E. (2012). Depression in inner city African American youth: A phenomenological study. *Journal of Child Family Studies.* https://www.kennedykrieger.org/sites/default/files/library/documents/patient-care/centers-and-programs/traumatic-stress-center/depression-african-american-youth-2012-dr-ofonedu.pdf

Raboteau, A. J. (1978). *Slave religion: The invisible institutions in the antiebellum south.* Glasgow Oxford University.

Rawick, G. P. (1972). *From sundown to sunup: The making of Black community.* Greenwood Press.

Rodriguez, N. (2007). Restorative justice at work: Examining the impact of restorative justice resolution on juvenile recidivism. *Crime & Delinquency, 53*(3), 355–379. https://doi.org/10.1177/0011128705285983

U.S. Department of Justice. (2019) *Report to Congress on the activities and operations of Public Integrity Section for 2019.* https://www.justice.gov/criminal-pin/file/1346061/download

Utsey, S. O., Giesbrecht, N., Hook, J., & Stanard, P. M. (2008). Cultural, socio-famial, and psychological resources that inhibit psychological distress in African Americans exposed to stressful life events and race-related stress. *Journal of Community Psychology, 55*(1), 49–62.

CHAPTER 3

Love and Learning Starts at Home

Wisdom From the Enslaved Person Narratives for the Family Domain

So it is better to speak

Remembering

we were never meant to survive.

—Audre Lorde, "A Litany for Survival"

The outside world told black kids when I was growing up that we weren't worth anything. But our parents said it wasn't so, and our churches and our schoolteachers said it wasn't so. They believed in us, and we, therefore, believed in ourselves.

—Marian Wright Edelman

Introduction

If we want guidelines focused on the resilience in young people with whom we have been working in the individual domain, then it becomes necessary to pay attention to the family in which they reside. This chapter describes the concerted, systematic, intentional fragmentation of families and their systems of support that began under slavery in America—and the unyielding resistance by enslaved human beings to counter such willful fragmentation. Such purposeful breakage sought to deny all Black family members, especially the young, the care, counsel, role models, and family-strengthening rituals that one associates with the protective factors provided by all families.

There were many egregious acts during slavery, perhaps none more egregious than the intentional decimation of the Black family as a primary strategy to sustain oppression and maintain White domination. It began in the woods of West African nations when villages were pillaged and men, women, and children were forced into the slave trade. The separation from community and family continued on the long walk to the coasts with the colonial fortresses that processed human chattel into ships through doors of no return as Africans made the transatlantic journey to New Orleans, South Carolina, and the Caribbean (Mustakeem, 2016; Rediker, 2007). Every step of the way, Africans fought and rebelled. What a sorrowful journey it had to have been! Imagine the wailing of children and mothers and fathers in the slave ships and, later, on the plantations as purposeful subjugation and oppression broke backs, bodies, and souls and tore families apart.

For anyone working in social work or education, we understand "trauma" inside families as divorces occur, a parent is imprisoned, or a beloved family member passes on before their time. However, imagine the level of trauma at play when another human being has encoded in law as well as culture and custom the right to purposely sell off your family member no matter the centrality, love, and support that they provide to their own children, spouse, and other family members (Gutman, 1976). This breakage was primarily targeted at Black men, robbing them of their defined traditional role within family units, but the suffering was experienced by women and children, fathers, mothers, grandparents, and kin (Holden, 2018).

Black women, on the other hand, were targeted not to be sold but to be raped (Feinstein, 2019). The breadth of sexual violence leading to the births of so many children could only occur if such practices were legal and both widespread and systematic. Again, rape by any means is violent and traumatizing. Yet modern rape in America is individualized and private. Under slavery the rape of Black women by their "masters" was prevalent and customary. How much more horrible an act with state support can one imagine?

We write this not to focus on the level of suffering such acts of separation and violence caused but to underscore for young people today that as horrific as this suffering was, it did not break our enslaved ancestors. There are many accounts of parents seeking separated children and spouses seeking separated spouses both during enslavement and in the years after it was ended (Gutman, 1976; Feinstein, 2019). Likewise, there was a lack of stigma attached to women forced through sexual violence to procreate more and more children (Liversey, 2017, p. 2).

As the narratives in this chapter make clear, the biological drive to reconnect with family upon emancipation was a moral imperative for separated loved ones.

Reuniting with biological kin was jubilee, a happiness beyond description. Reunification solidified the family unit, the building block of the community, and is the only way that Black folk today can say with any certainty on whose shoulders they stand. People once enslaved have strong memories of their mother's love, of their father's strength, of efforts to be reunited. Knowing such perseverance to reconnect under such hardship is a necessary antidote to popular messaging of broken families and the presumed pathology of the single-parent household (Coates, 2015; Moynihan, 1965).

One cannot sugarcoat either the past horror or the carrying out of such brutal policies throughout American history. As is well known, the attempts to annihilate the Black family begun under slavery later gave rise to further family fragmentation policies in America well into the 20th century. Indeed, the welfare policies of the 1950s and 1960s forbade men to live with their spouses if they were to receive welfare (Jansson, 2018). From the 1990s to today there have been further attempts at breakage through mass incarceration that was targeted disproportionately at men of color (Coates, 2015). And yet, despite this truth, cohesive Black families have remained a constant entity during bondage and throughout American history. As horrific and degrading as their conditions were, the enslaved people carried within them the profound awareness that through a Black family one could be emboldened to provide proper care to the young, wise counsel between the generations, positive role models, and value of rituals begun generations ago in West African villages. Black families adapted—with kin from next door, aunts and uncles from life-long friendship, and sought-after relatives ripped apart from one planation to the next—and formed strong bonds despite the "masters'" unyielding efforts to deny their ability to constitute themselves as a living unit strengthened through love, connection, and commitment.

Protective Factors in the Domain of the Family

Enslavers were usually aware of and, ironically, considered themselves strong supporters of enslaved families. Motivated by both a paternalistic concern for the well-being of their "people" and a calculating regard for their own economic interest, slaveowners paid increasing attention to the family lives of their enslaved. The actions of the enslavers were in many ways contradictory; they not only supported enslaved families but also disrupted them through forced separations and forced sex (Feinstein, 2019; Kolchin, 1993). Imagine not being certain of who you are or where your people come from, as in the case of Anthony Taylor from Arkansas: "I don't know the names of my father's people, they was sole in slavery."[1]

The fewest number of narrative excerpts in this study's sample related to family resilience. Even under the best of situations, Kolchin (1993) asserts that enslaved families lacked the institutional and legal support enjoyed by those who were free, and in extreme cases enslavers could not only hinder but also prevent the development of normal family relations.

America Morgan from Indiana lost her mother to a whipping from "ole massa"; she said that "she was left motherless to face a frowning world."[2]

At the same time, families provided a crucial if fragile buffer, shielding the enslaved people from the worst rigors of slavery (Blassingame, 1979; Kolchin, 1993). The research in this study concluded that enslaved families characterized by familial connections to (a) care, (b) counsel, (c) positive role models, and (d) rituals offered the best protections from the trauma of slavery. Such protective factors can continue to be used for our young people today.

Care Defined as Assistance in Time of Need, Love, Support, and Appropriate Caretaking

If childhood was a special time for enslaved children, it was because their parents made it so. They stood between them and enslavers who sought to control them psychologically and to break their wills to resist (Blassingame, 1979; King 1995). Many enslaved people routinely slipped off the plantation for a rest from plantation work. Sometimes the enslaved person ran away and while they were fugitives were dependent on aid from other enslaved families.

Henry Wright from Georgia reported that "while a fugitive he slept in the woods eating wild berries etc. sometimes he slipped to the plantation of his mother or that of his father where he was able to secure food."[3] Please note that this family had been split in not two but three, and yet they risked their lives to stay connected: mother to son, father to son.

Some enslaved men and women had near-death experiences and were fortunate enough to have a family member nearby to provide assistance. George Jackson from Ohio also received life-saving assistance; he can remember when "[his] brother Henry pulled [him] out of de fire."[4]

Alternatively, in the absence of children, enslaved women prayed for a good man to ease the strain of life on the plantation. Gracie Mitchell from Arkansas talked about the importance of her husband's support: "I was a motherless chile but the Lord made up for it by givin' me a good husband and I don't want for anything."[5] Lasting love between two people can heal even in the most trying of conditions.

Many enslaved men and women talked about the unconditional love and support they received from mothers and fathers. Willis Williams from Florida remarked on the care his mother provided: "His mother saw to it that her children were well fed."[6]

Susan Matthews from Georgia said, "After de war wuz over my pa, he comed up to our house and got my ma and all us chillen an carries us down to his marster's place. My pa wuz a hard worker an we helped him an in a few years he bought a little piece of land an he owned it till he died."[7] *Again, notice the separation did not deter this man from finding and reconnecting to his family.*

Marion Johnson from Arkansas remarked on the ingenuity of his mother when faced with a medical emergency. He recalls, "I members one time I got a long splinter in my foot and couldn't get it out, so my mammy bound a piece of fat meat round my foot and let it stay bout a couple days, then the splinter come out real easy like."[8]

That was a lesson of love that no doubt represented a remedy passed down from older generations and stayed with him throughout his life. Likewise, Dan Bogie from Kentucky recalled a very early memory in slavery when responding to questions from the WPA agent: "I remembers the cradle I was placed in where my mama would rock me and she used to sit and sing in the evening."[9]

Enslaved Person Narrative Excerpt

Willis Williams, 81 years old and from Florida, had vivid memories about his mother growing up in slavery. He talked about the unconditional love and support he received from his mother. He remarked on the care his mother provided: "His mother saw to it that her children were well fed." And he felt her love through the good food she prepared. She was the cook in the enslaver's house and he said, "I felt like I was always eating at the master's table."[10] That meant that he was eating well.

Barbara's Client Example

Darnell, 13 years old, had been in and out of foster care since his birth. His mother was a poly-substance user and was in and out of jail for theft and other crimes. She made attempts at treatment but relapsed and spiraled out of control with her addiction and her behaviors. There were no other family members to assume temporary or permanent custody and care of her son. Consequently, her son was removed from her care due to neglect and abuse. He was born addicted to crack cocaine and had a rough start in life as a premature and undernourished baby.

Darnell was in and out of therapy and counseling for years as he struggled with unexpressed emotions and desperately wanted the love and care of his biological mother. When I met Darnell he had been living with his current foster parents for 4 years and was thriving and doing well in school and in social relations. The child protection agency was making a plan for permanency for Darnell and referred him to a family resource center for family support while the foster parents were being processed for becoming adoptive parents. Darnell and the soon-to-be adoptive parents received case management and counseling services as well as engagement services with other foster families to validate the next steps they were taking to become a permanent family. Like Mr. Williams, Darnell would often remark about the nice home he lived in, the desk he had to study at, the stability of the home, and the ways his basic needs were being met. He was learning how to cope with loss of the connection to his biological mother and was learning about addiction and the despair that is associated with the condition. He often times remarked how fortunate he was to finally have the love and concern of parental figures. He wrote moving accounts of his journey in his adoption scrapbook. He beamed like the sun the day the adoption was completed, and he took the name of his new parents. He also vowed to stay connected with his own birth mother when he was old enough to make contact with her.

Mr. Williams's and Darnell's stories affirm that one of the core functions of family, whether during bondage or during the harsh reality of urban life in the 21st century, is to aid in meeting the basic needs of children.

Deborah's Educational Example

Syreeta, a 17-year-old, had spent her previous 7 years in foster care. She had absolutely no trouble speaking her mind and did so with a quickness that rivaled Apollo's arrow headed for its intended target. Over the years many of Syreeta's case workers found this open-minded sharing one-sided, largely due to their insurmountable caseloads. They simply did not have the time or the human bandwidth to manage the kind of truly present and attentive listening she required. While this added to her anger at the general condition of being in care, she did not hesitate to say what she felt she needed to have heard.

She broadened her potential audience by joining as many activities as possible. Her case workers would often find her new or even trial programming in a continuous effort to bolster foster care youth in place of the familial and community support that was stripped from them when they entered care.

One such program brought foster care youth together in a large educational forum to give audience to their voice(s). Youth were invited to share their thoughts on a number of issues, including their placement in foster homes. This was a contentious issue, as many of the youth had a great deal to say, including Syretta. Her major concern was that she was raised in a home where they did not shy away from eating pork. When she entered foster care she was placed with a family that did not believe in eating pork, a placement she believed unfairly ignored her familial culture. Her comments were met with a number of nodding heads affirming her sentiments as true.

Many of the organizers were also taking note. Having been heard by others ignited Syretta's need to express similar sentiments. However, the audience contained over 100 youth, and the organizers simply did not expect the kind of collective outpouring the youth offered. In an effort to tap into as many issues/concerns from as many as possible, Syretta and others who had already had their voices heard were asked to step back and give others a chance.

As the next session was beginning with new participants on stage, Syretta became agitated, so much so that she pulled on the arm of her case worker and told her that she knew the young man speaking. The case worker nodded and gestured to her to sit down quietly.

Syretta sat down but could not stay down. She approached the caseworker again, and said, "Please; I know that person speaking." Giving into Syretta's sense of urgency, the case worker took her over to the young man who had just spoken.

He turned and looked at her, she said, "Tim," and he said, "Syretta"; they hugged, shared tears, and finally she said to the case worker: "This is my brother. I haven't seen him for 7 years."

They were sent to separate foster care homes but had vowed to never be separated again. As they were both in their late teens, this connection could be managed. And like enslaved people before them, their separation as young children could not alter their family bond. Despite the fragmentation wrought by foster care, they have been reunited ever since.

Counsel Defined as Instructive, Providing Guidance and Structure to the Rearing of Family Members and Preventing Risky Behaviors

To avoid difficulties, enslaved children were reliant on the counsel of their older siblings, parents, and other older relatives who resided in the quarters. Martin Jackson from Texas said, "My father was always counseling me and he said 'everyman has to serve god under his own vine and fig tree.' He kept pointing out that, 'the war wasn't going to last forever, but that our forever was going to be spent living among the Southerners after they got licked.'"[11]

Family members provided counsel toward the development of good character. Bill Heard from Georgia sheds some light on the kind of structure his family reared him in by comparing his rearing in slavery with his observations of young people being raised in the 20th century: "Funerals warn't so common den as now 'cause folks didn't die out so fast dem days. Dey tuk better keer of deyselfs, at right, wuked hard, and went to bed at night 'stid of folks runs 'round now; dier mammies and daddies never knows whar dey is."[12]

The same goes for Warren Taylor from Arkansas, who offers additional instruction on the counsel of young people from his own upbringing: "The parents don't teach the children, and the children can't amount to anything. If children are not taught to work, they will never have nothing."[13]

Jennie Kendricks from Georgia references the preventative nature of the family counseling experience; she said, "My mother always see to it that her children had sufficient to eat so that they would not have to steal and would therefore grow up to be honorable."[14]

The elders were a source of counsel to the next generation of enslaved people, passing on wisdom and knowhow to the younger enslaved people. Some, because of their age, had special favor in the eyes of the enslavers; some, not. Many possessed knowledge about medicines and remedies. The role of the elder in the enslaved family is recounted. Willis Williams from Florida remembers his granny; he says, "I spent much time around the grannies during slavery and learned much about herbs and roots and how they were used to cure all manner of ills."[15]

Enslaved Person Narrative Excerpt

Isaac Stier is 99 years old and from Lauderdale County, Natchez, Mississippi. Mr. Stier remembered being on a large plantation with about 90 enslaved people. He remembered the hardships during the Civil War, his hunger and the fear of those "ungodly times," and his parents telling him how to be happy with the way life was and to be patient for change to happen. He was comparing his upbringing to his observations about Black youth in the 1930s. He said, "Dis generation aint got much sens. Dey's tryin' to git somewhere too fas'. None of 'em is sat'fied wid plain livin'. Dey wants too much. Nobody needs more dan dey can use, nohow."[16] He expressed that their impatience with the way things are and their wanting things rather than being satisfied with the basics in life was bad for them.

Barbara's Client Example

Barry, a 16-year-old, and his single mother began family therapy around some of his defiant behaviors and his constant angry responses when his mother put limits on his demands for things. His mother was laid off from her job, and she took another job that provided significantly less in salary. Barry had a difficult time with the adjustment to the new budget. He and his mother were arguing more and more. Mom was shopping at different stores for sales. He felt embarrassed about his shoes and his clothes. He wanted more take-out foods. Cable TV was cut back. Prepaid minutes on his phone were cut back. Barry was very angry at his mom and became verbally abusive toward her and his younger sibling. Over time, in family therapy, both were better able to verbalize their frustration and resentments to the financial stress.

Just as Mr. Stier preached, with patience they learned and practiced alternatives to verbal frustration and agreed to work on communication. Neither wanted to injure or hurt the other. They loved each other. They made a contract and agreements about communicating better about purchasing items. Barry became financially literate as his mom became more transparent about family finances after participating in a school-based program aimed at increasing financial literacy. Not unlike what Mr. Stier and his parents learned and practiced while enslaved, he learned the hard truth about the high cost of material goods. He also learned the difference between things he needed and things he wanted. Barry got motivated to take a job at a local movie theater so that he could meet some of his own needs to take the burden off his mother. His mother agreed to allow him to keep most of the money he earned for his own purposes. He also set up a savings account at a local bank.

Deborah's Educational Example

Plato's arrival in America was hardly an immigrant's dream: his father simply dropped him off at the nearest church and fled, never to be seen again. (Plato never knew his mother.) At the age of 7, neither knowing a word of English nor where he was, he ended up in 11 different foster homes over the next 10 years. At the same time, he somehow never lost his bright and optimistic outlook and managed to work toward completion of school, even though he had been diagnosed with ADHD.

Plato was enrolled in a special after-school program that emphasized one-on-one mentoring and tutoring, and I made sure he was assigned a tutor who had been an immigrant himself. He and Robin hit it off immediately, and Robin, even though he was only an associate commissioner, made time weekly to help tutor him.

It turned out that Plato had a passion for music and set a career goal to become a successful DJ. His tutor worked with this goal and combined it to the educational skill development needed for Plato to graduate by helping him create a business plan and by completing a course on entrepreneurship. This mix of problem solving, some financial literacy, and writing helped Plato both start his career and complete his high school degree.

A few years later, I attended a lavish wedding party and was thrilled to see none other than Plato, now dressed sharply in a three-piece suit, complete with tie. He spotted me as well, and he proudly handed me his embossed business card. Plato had used his tutoring well: He was a professional DJ, able to make a living on his own and was still in contact with his tutor.

Models Defined as Positive Examples for Imitation or Emulation

Enslaved children, like all children, learn behaviors from their primary reference group—namely, parents. Parents during enslavement oftentimes made very difficult decisions that on their face seem unexplainable. For example, a family decides to stay on the plantation after freedom. What would compel a mother to suppress the impulse to be free? Perhaps the impulse to survive as a family is a greater end. Wiley Childress from Tennessee provides evidence of this protective factor; he said, "W'en we all wuz freed we had nuthin en no place ter go, so dat mah mammy lived wid our Missus five y'ars longer."[17]

Rosaline Rogers from Indiana talks about the trade-off of maintaining family versus leaving the plantation as a free woman: "At the close of the war, I was given my choice of staying on the same plantation, working on shares, or taking my family away, letting them out for their food and clothes. I decided to stay on that way; I could have my children with me."[18]

Another woman, Delia Garlic from the state of Alabama, said, "When we knowed we wuz free, everybody wanted to git out. De rule wuz dat if you stayed in yo' cabin you could keep it, but if you lef' you los' it. My husband wuz workin' at W (a neighboring plantation) an' he slipped in and' out so us could keep on livin' in de cabin."[19] He sacrificed living full time with his family so as not to place the entire family in jeopardy of losing their housing.

Not unlike so many stories one hears from professional athletes, many of the enslaved people in the sample attribute much of their survival story to the strength of their mothers. James Lucas from Mississippi said, “My mammy sho’ was healthy and strong.”[20]

And he also saw the limits of materialism: “The longer I lives de plainer I see dat it ain’ right to want mo’ den you can use.”[21]

Bill Heard from Georgia expressed two important values: “Folks don’t teach chillum right, and dey don’t make dem go to church lak dey should oughta.”[22] He asserted that education and religion are two important values for adults to model for their children. This statement underscores the importance of parents being positive role models for their children, in temperament and in deeds.

Enslaved Person Narrative Excerpt

Bill Heard, 73 years old, was a blacksmith and owned his own shop when the Federal Writers’ Project agent located him for the interview. He was born in Elbert County, Georgia, and was enslaved with over 125 other enslaved people on the plantation. Surprisingly, he often referred to slavery as “dem good old days” because he felt Black people helped one another out more then. He learned the value of working hard and getting religion and education both during bondage and when he was freed. He said, “Folks don’t teach chillun right and dey don’t make dem go to church lak dey should oughta.”[23] His implication was that parents needed to emulate the values his parents taught him about hard work, keeping faith, and acting right.

Barbara’s Client Example

Donna, a 13-year-old freshman, and her mother were referred for counseling services after she got into an altercation with another student in the classroom. She also cursed the teacher out when he intervened to restore order in the class. Donna was sent to the disciplinarian at the school. The vice principal called her mother, who arrived to the school quickly, as the family home was within blocks of the school. When her mom arrived, within minutes she began to curse at the school staff in the presence of her daughter. It seemed the apple didn’t fall far from the tree in regard to the way to communicate frustration and upset to others.

We successfully managed to get the mom to agree to family counseling with her daughter to address aggressive and inappropriate behaviors in school and the difficulty Donna was having with adjusting to high school. Emphasis in counseling with the mom was imperative for modeling appropriate communication, coping, and behaviors. The mom was defensive but also wanted so much for her daughter to have a better life than she was having. She loved her daughter. She felt she was teaching her daughter how to live in mean streets. The mom and Donna had experienced loss and witnessed violence in the community. Like Mr. Heard, Donna’s mom was not afraid of hard work. She maintained involvement in a parent support group for the duration of the school year, and both she and her daughter utilized a variety of newly learned coping, communication, and distress tolerance skills. Donna was also given extra support for her academic work, as a learning disability had been identified through testing, and accommodations in the classroom helped her have greater success in school. The inability to master certain competencies in class was the root of much of her frustration and the butt of some bullying from classmates. With the effort of a blacksmith, Donna's mom changed some of her behaviors and attitudes, and eventually, so did her daughter. The most important change was in engaging the school staff, building relationships with teachers, counselors, and administrators. She developed greater trust in a system that she felt cared little about her or her daughter.

Deborah's Educational Example

Cedric, a tall, brown-skinned young student, was often characterized as being the class clown. This was quite the distinction in his fifth-grade class, as there were many outspoken students similar to him in appearance, and yet it appeared that he managed without too much effort to out clown them all. Or at least that was the finding of his teacher. Perhaps his teacher simply had her fill of class clowns, especially so early in the school year, and if that was the case, they all should have benefitted from the same or similar discipline that he was afforded. And since many of them were his friends (after all, he did practice a kind of "honor" among class clowns), he learned that he was singled out for his behavior and his parents were the only ones called into school. His parents were hard-working Black parents who instilled what they believed to be honor and decency in their children.

Cedric's mother, knowing how she and his father intentionally raised their children in preparation to successfully assimilate as contributing citizens, did not appreciate being summoned to the school to answer for Cedric's behavior. That was not acceptable for her children. Cedric's mother appeared at the school as representing both parents. His father's work schedule did not permit him to take time away from work, and there really was no need for both of them to appear. He knew he and his wife were in total agreement when it came to raising their children. Surprised, Cedric's mother found herself escorted to the principal's office, where the principal and Cedric's teacher greeted her. Cedric sat with hands crossed in his lap and with little expression otherwise. He knew his mother was not at all happy with being summoned to the principal's office for the sole purpose of defending her son's behavior in the classroom. She respected educators; however, she also knew her son, so she listened quietly as the teacher presented the story of Cedric's behavior.

Once the events were fully chronicled, she simply asked, "Have you tested him, and if so, what did the assessments reveal?" The teacher answered, "Yes, we have, and he did score quite high, which we thought was a mistake given his acting-out behavior." The principal and the teacher looked at each other, and the principal asked, "Why are you asking?" Cedric's mother stated that she is fully aware that her son may act out in class and asked if they considered that he might simply be bored and that he might benefit from a more accelerated curriculum, especially given that he scored well on the assessments they administered. The teacher looked to the principal, perhaps seeking a response in support of the current pedagogical practices that she and other teachers were instructed to use.

The principal looked at Cedric's mother and asked, "If you don't mind, would you please tell us what you do?" Cedric's mother responded, "I am the principal of an elementary school." The room became suddenly quiet. The meeting ended with the understanding that Cedric's test results would be accepted and that consideration for a more accelerated placement would be considered. When they were clear of the school building, Cedric's mother stopped midstep, turned him to face her, and reassured him that just because some teachers and educators do not believe or expect that you have what it takes to succeed and that you are smart, you will always have to remember that you are and keep proving it on all on the tests they throw at you.

Cedric's mother changed the school's approach on how they track and move students of color, with the possibility that they, too, may not only benefit from but also qualify for an enriched pedagogical approach. And like the enslaved man in Mississippi, Cedric knew without fail that his mom was indeed healthy and strong.

Rituals Defined as Customarily Repeated Actions, Rites, Traditions, or Celebrations

The agents from the WPA specifically asked about rituals (weddings/funerals/ birthing), celebrations, and holidays as a matter of routine; therefore, virtually every narrative makes mention of what special foods the enslaver provided during these special occasions and the temporary reprieve from slave work (unless you were the cook and wait servants). The enslaved person used this time to reconnect with family members and conduct activities to maintain the family. Many enslaved men and women recounted life after working for "master"—Saturday night and Sundays.

Others talked about attending church together as a family. Lucindia Washington from Alabama reported on the routine of attending Sunday church as a family before having a big feast with the family: "Us'd go to church wid de white folks on Sunday and sit in de back, an' den we go home an' eat a big Sunday meal."[24]

Jane Sutton from Mississippi recalled the routine of dressing up for Sunday church on the plantation and the good feelings she and her family felt preparing for attending church: "When us dress' up in Sund'y clo'es us had caliker dresses. Dey sho' was pretty."[25]

There weren't many happy memories, says Horace Overstreet from Texas, but he recalled a regular weekend ritual that seemed to temper the harshness of bondage. He fondly remembered a good time with his family when he said, "Seemed like my folks was happy when de starts dancin.'"[26]

Regarding marriage, Camilla Jackson from Georgia recalled that "she married immediately after freedom and proudly spoke of being the first person to wed in the "Big Bethel Church."[27] She wanted so much to have the ritual akin to the ritual of White families. More common, however, is the broom-jumping ritual of enslaved families that they carried with them from West Africa. James Boulton from Georgia said, "Folkses didn' make no big todo over weddings like they do now, when slave got married they jus' laid down the broom on the floor and the couple jined hands and jumped back-uds over the broomstick."[28] These rituals and valued celebrations helped to provide and/or establish critical reference group bonding experiences that helped to stave off the indignity of bondage.

Enslaved Person Narrative Excerpt

Anthony Taylor from Arkansas said he and his family were owned by "old man Bullocks." He remembered that after the war was over and he and his family stayed on the plantation, earning 10 cents a day, when he left off the plantation he had to have a pass. He recalled watching his grandparents and his parents being whipped.

The enslaved people used time to reconnect with family members and conducted activities to maintain the family. Mr. Anthony Taylor expressed the importance of Sunday breakfast: "We would work hard all the week talkin' 'bout what good biscuits we'd have come every Sunday morning when the family was together 'round the table."[29] That ritual sustained them while in slavery and in the many years to follow as sharecroppers and freed people.

Barbara's Client Example

Angela, 13 years old, was articulate, smart, and forward thinking. She had a close relationship with her mother. Then her mother decided to go to school to get her associate degree, and Angela often times became the primary caretaker of her younger sister. She had built up resentments about the change because it meant she couldn't hang with her own friends. She was conflicted. She loved her little sister. And she was missing family time with her mom. This was making her angry and sad. Her mom agreed to participate in family counseling with her daughter, and after a series of family-sculpting exercises, the picture of her mom's absence in the home became very clear. Both children were able to verbalize their need for more attention and time with their mom.

Not unlike Mr. Taylor's pleasure in the weekly ritual of Sunday family breakfasts, the family developed a weekly family time ritual and spent sessions creating the experience that centered around home-cooked meals and movie time/play time at least one time a week. This became a time that family came first and there were agreed-on check-ins on the activities, feelings, and concerns of each of them. After 3 months of implementing this ritual 'round the table, Angela and her mother endorsed feeling better, happier, and more connected.

Deborah's Educational Example

Grant had been a solid student when in elementary and middle school, but he was often sullen and angry in high school. In the cafeteria he sat alone, usually with a scowl on his face, staring at his uneaten food. I was puzzled by this, given his earlier success, and met with Grant to talk with him. It turned out that his family was now struggling financially. He didn't feel he could eat: "I feel like if I eat lunch, my (younger) brother and sister won't eat. They have to eat." Grant had converted his family's stressors into the false belief that ending his own hunger through cafeteria food was harming his younger siblings.

I created a simple solution based on what became our daily ritual: I would hand him my lunch (provided through the school), which he would eat. In turn, he would take his own lunch and provide it to his family. While we also worked to help his family overcome hunger, this ritual provided Grant with the means to moderate his stress, sustain himself, and provide for his beloved younger brother and sister. Like the formerly enslaved woman from Georgia, he made sure he provided for family members through enormous effort.

Implications for Social Workers and Educators Regarding Familial Connections for Black Americans

Those enslaved men and women who had familial connections to care, counsel, role models, and rituals were afforded additional protections from the brutality of bondage. In addition to the operation of individual coping strengths, African American youth from high-risk environments can benefit from more protections related to family factors. These protective factors represent universal functions of families and qualities related to the reality of racism and African American culture.

Providing care, love, and support to children is a universal function of a healthy, functioning family. Teenagers continue to crave the love and care of their parents, as they did when they were younger children. Such love and care are affirmations of personhood. Teens push parents away as a normal part of adolescence, but teens want their parent to take an interest in their interests. It can be a source of ongoing strength that feeds personal resilience. Another universal function of family is to be the laboratory for learning. Teens continue to take cues from adults about how to handle situations, how to respond to pressure, and how to be in relationships, as well as about more concrete things such as how to cook, manage an apartment/home, or provide care to a younger sibling. Teens connect to parents for encouragement to succeed in school and in life, and they are watching the habits and attitudes of their caregivers. They look to parents as role models for learning so that they can become prepared to deal with life outside the home.

Part of the learning parents transmit to their teens is to provide counsel about how to deal with the realities of life—oftentimes, the more harsh realities of life. Today's teens are under so much more pressure than many of us can imagine. They rely on trusted mentoring from their family to assist with coping with the demands of their lives. This is really the transmission of intergenerational wisdom to teens about how to live in Black skin in White America, and the counseling is also instructive about how to make it despite the disadvantage. The counseling is about the rules of the game, the unfairness of it all, and some coaching about how to play the game despite that reality. The relationship allows for additional advice about risky behaviors and rudimentary behavioral analysis about the pros and cons of ill-advised actions.

There are other ways to teach teens life lessons besides counseling. Establishing unique and culturally inherited rituals can help to support resilience. There is structure and reliability in regular rituals within a family—how to celebrate birthdays, holidays, funerals, weddings, family meetings, menstruation celebration, showers, serving Sunday dinner, family reunions, going to church, girls' night out. Whatever the ritual is, teens gain a sense of security and widening the familial net of support within and for the family. Rituals are anchors for the family that promote connections and togetherness. Sometimes parents and kids alike experience a feeling of alienation and loneliness related to the pressures of day-to-day survival, and rituals can help to shift the feeling to one of mutuality, kinship, and support. This provides a critical layer of protection for all children in the home from the deleterious effects of environmental stress.

For both family practice and education, the approach to this level of intervention is also about empowerment and skill building. Parents and caregivers need support and training on how to provide care, counsel, learning, modeling, and other rituals. The lesson from the enslaved person narratives is that the Black family has always been under assault, but somehow adaptations and adjustments are made by widening the circle of family members so that the good of all can be served.

The truth is sometimes our clients and students are in families that for both structural and interpersonal reasons do not have the ability to provide the full measure of what is needed for their children. Many of the parents of the teenagers we see are young themselves and have unresolved needs of their own that interfere with their ability to parent effectively. Dialectically speaking, they are doing the best they can, but they need to change some things about the way they parent. As our 80 years of experience make clear, we can love all our families, and yet some families are troubled, and some live in home environments that are toxic and at times dangerous.

The aim of intervention at this level is identify the "elder" or "elders" in the family system (as defined by the youth) who can provide the best support and counseling to the youth while parents participate in their own self-improvement activity. These one or more individuals can be given proxy to stand in for parents in arenas where their child needs support. This is especially important for school and other community agencies or organizations, as communications between systems and caregivers is important for effective service delivery.

The practitioner or teacher can assist with the building of concrete skills that can help to relieve some stress in the home environment around effective communication, conflict resolution, time management, and other interpersonal skills related to behavioral management. From the standpoint of cultural axiology, it is important to frame practice objectives from a member–member vantage point. This includes assisting parents with the implementation of new rituals to support the growth and maturity of the children in the home.

Additionally, the practitioner can help increase parents' skills in advocating for resources in the larger environment to help relieve some of the stress related to poverty and other factors. When working with family systems, other professional resources may need to be activated through formal and informal referral systems. The wider the base of support, combined with the skill building of the parents, the better the chance that youth will gain the benefits of the protective factors from the family domain.

The Sankofa Guidance for Practitioners and Educators: Working with Families

1. Step outside of the family box. In this domain you have to step outside of the box; you must abandon your preconceived notions about what constitutes a family. Ask the adolescent who they consider a family. Who do they consider their role models? Who do they consider the elders? Perhaps a minister or coach or a teacher, neighbor, or another provider will be recruited for participation in this domain on behalf of the adolescent.

2. Remember intergenerational transmission of trauma. It's important to remember the transmission of intergenerational trauma at this point and in this domain because that trauma impacts the psychological mindedness of the caregiver/parent and their ability to support the healing of their teen child. We have to attend to the wellness of the parent as well as the child. Consider the shame of the parent, and consider their deep desire to be well and to be able to help and simply not being up to the task; empathy and compassion are the hallmarks of practice in this domain.

This means that it's critical to be able to build a relationship with the parent/guardian and to gently and skillfully engage with them on their own path to healing. This may require referrals for their own counseling to deal with unresolved trauma. This is especially true for parents who were teen parents. It's important to connect them to their own resources and to work on their individual healing as you also work on family engagement, family cohesion, and family healing.

3. Don't let adults "parentify" their kids. Parents, please stop calling your 13-year-old son the man of the house. He isn't a man. He is a teen! Allow him to be a teen. Let him play. Let him make mistakes. Don't rush him into adult situations. Stop making an older daughter the mother to her other siblings. Allow her to play. Allow her to have time for after-school programs. Allow her to have time to have other relationships with friends. Monitor how much adult business people are sharing with their teens. Open adult stress stresses children out!

4. Support children in their chosen activities. Help parents and other adult kin understand that if their teen plays football, they should try to get to a game. If their teen is on the debate team, they should try to get to a debate match. Tell parents to do their best to take an interest in their children's activities and participate in their lives. Tell them to go to those parent–teacher conferences, and if they can't, encourage them to arrange for some other family member to be there in their absence.

5. Start with basic needs. Remember Maslow's hierarchy of needs in this domain. Rapid assessment of basic needs is critical. Is there food in the refrigerator? Are the lights on? Are there beds? Is the water running? Is there evidence of any violence, physical abuse, or neglect?

6. Strengthen communication. What is the baseline level of communication between members of the family? Pay attention to spatial alignments and patterns of interruptions and who has control of shaping the dynamics in the family.

As educators and social workers, we need to be in the learner mode and not be judges as we work together with our Black families, and we need to do so through a lens of the strength they hold and not assign or presuppose limitations on growth based on skin color. Turn off the TV/electronic gadgets. Make time for face-to-face communication. Talk about real stuff, such as a menstrual cycles and how to deal with police. This is a time for education and empowerment. Knowledge is power.

7. Focus on family dynamics. Healthy children come from healthy families. According to the American Academy of Pediatrics (2015), there are several characteristics that are generally identified with a well-functioning family. Some include support; love and caring for other family members; providing security and a sense of belonging; open communication; and making each person within the family feel important, valued, respected, and esteemed. These qualities are universal qualities of healthy families. It is true for White families and Black families. Our children need to be safe in their own homes. Unsupervised children are at risk for incest and abuse. It is important to monitor for the safety of our children. It is okay to spoil our children with love.

8. Build relationships with people in different cultural groups. There is no difference beyond the cosmetics in the Black home versus the White home. But how many White people cross over and have the experience of engagement with a Black family in their home? Not enough? If we dared to engage and to cross over and participate in the intimate space of our kitchen tables and living rooms with each other, we would go a long way in fostering better relationships and understanding about Black youth and Black families. We need more open doors and more opportunities to connect. When that happens we will see that we indeed share the common desire to have families that sustain and nurture our dreams and help us cope with all the experiences that living life throws our way.

Endnotes

Excerpts from the Federal Writers' Project Slave Narrative (FWPSN) Collection

1. FWPSN, Arkansas, Part 6, p. 259
2. FWPSN, Indiana, p. 141
3. FWPSN, Georgia, Part 4, p. 202
4. FWPSN, Ohio, p. 45
5. FWPSN, Arkansas, Part 5, p. 108
6. FWPSN, Florida, p. 348
7. FWPSN, Georgia, Part 3, p. 117
8. FWPSN, Arkansas, Part 4, p. 116
9. FWPSN, Kentucky, p. 1
10. FWPSN, Florida, p. 348
11. FWPSN, Texas, Part 2, p. 189
12. FWPSN, Georgia, Part 2, p. 141
13. FWPSN, Arkansas, Part 6, p. 278
14. FWPSN, Georgia, Part 3, p. 3
15. FWPSN, Florida, pp. 353–354
16. FWPSN, Mississippi, p. 150
17. FWPSN, Tennessee, p. 9
18. FWPSN, Indiana, p. 165
19. FWPSN, Alabama, p. 132
20. FWPSN, Mississippi, p. 91
21. FWPSN, Mississippi, p. 99
22. FWPSN, Georgia, Part 2, p. 141
23. FWPSN, Georgia, Part 2, p. 141
24. FWPSN, Alabama, p. 410
25. FWPSN, Mississippi, p. 152
26. FWPSN, Texas, Part 3, p. 160
27. FWPSN, Georgia, Part 2, p. 298
28. FWPSN, Georgia, Part 1, p. 101
29. FWPSN, Arkansas, Part 6, p. 262

References

American Academy of Pediatrics. (2015). *Normal family functioning.* https://www.healthychildren.org/English/family-life/family-dynamics/Pages/Normal-Family-Functioning.aspx

Blassingame, J. W. (1979). *The slave community: Plantation life in the antebellum South.* Oxford University Press.

Coates, T. (2015, October). The Black family in the age of mass incarceration. *The Atlantic.* https://www.theatlantic.com/magazine/archive/2015/10/the-black-family-in-the-age-of-mass-incarceration/403246/

Feinstein, R. (2019). *When rape was Legal: The untold history of sexual violence during slavery.* Routledge.

Gutman, H. (1976). *The Black family in slavery and freedom 1750–1925.* Pantheon.

Holden, V. (2018, July 25). *Slavery and America's legacy of family separation.* Black Perspectives. https://www.aaihs.org/slavery-and-americas-legacy-of-family-separation/

Jansson, B. (2018). *Becoming an effective policy advocate: From policy practice to social justice.* Brooks/Cole.

King, W. (1995). *Stolen childhood: Slave youth in 19th-century America.* Indiana University Press.

Kolchin, P. (1993). *American slavery: 1619-1877.* Hill and Wang.

Livesey, A. (2017). Conceived in violence: Enslaved mothers and children born of rape in nineteenth-century Louisiana. *Slavery & Abolition, 38*(2), 373–391. https://researchonline.ljmu.ac.uk/id/eprint/9836/3/Conceived%20in%20Violence%20Enslaved%20Mothers%20and%20Children%20Born%20of%20Rape%20in%20Nineteenth-Century%20Louisiana.pdf

Myonihan, D. (1965). *The Negro family: The case for national action.* Office of Policy Planning and Research, U.S. Department of Labor. http://dol.gov/oasam/programs/history/webid-moynihan.htm

Mustakeem, S. (2016). *Slavery at sea: Terror, sex, and sickness in the Middle Passage.* University of Illinois Press.

Rediker, M. (2007). *The slave ship: A human story.* Viking.

CHAPTER 4

I Am Because You Are

Wisdom From the Enslaved Person Narratives for the Black Community Domain

Strong communities are born out of individuals being their best selves.

—Leanne Betasamosake Simpson

It is in collectivities that we find reservoirs of hope and optimism.

—Angela Y. Davis

Introduction

When one thinks of "community," what comes to mind are likely ideas of a group of people sharing resources and common interests, providing mutual support, and creating opportunities for socialization and economic well-being (Burghardt, 2014; Gouldner, 1978; Homan, 2017). Constructed into the idea of community are elements of autonomy and some mix of interdependence to allow a person's development of their own common culture and norms that help to provide common understanding and meaning across generations. Think of your local community—whether a rural farming community outside Des Moines, Iowa, or the urban enclave of Far Rockaways of Queens, New York—and immediate associations are easily made. Mention "community" in such settings, and culture, values, activities, and rituals can easily be defined.

Now travel back in time to Georgia or Louisiana, where "enslavers" purposely sought to limit common connections of the Africans living among them, consciously filling their slave ships with people from different tribes, ethnicities, and languages

(Desroches, 1997; Etis & Richardson, 2015). By forcing them to adapt only to the lash of the southern plantation (and, for over 100, the farms of the North), the goal was not community but disconnection, leading to servitude and a diminished self-identity (McKenna, 2021). All the common forms of civic connection afforded even White working-class men—ale houses for socializing, meeting houses for service, schooling for their sons (and an occasional daughter)—were not simply denied them; to have openly attempted group association, let alone community creation, was met with whippings and even death.

And yet a sense of a unique Black community solidarity nevertheless managed to be formed regardless of enslavement. This research's findings reinforce, in seemingly small snippets and asides, other research that reveals the myriad ways enslaved Black Americans forged common connection. First, the enslaved Africans did not appear on our shores as broken empty slates to be filled with White forms of domination. They carried with them rituals, for example, marriage rituals as well as the practice of "ring shout" in religious ceremonies that gave rise to the vibrant call-and-response tradition found in almost all African American churches (Rogers, 2006), as well as fully emersed baptisms that were modeled after African religious traditions. Applying such practices to every ethnic group and tribe brought its own unifying purpose to enslaved Africans—as unintended as it was (Ntloedibe, 2019).

They arrived with their music as well, through the oldest of instruments: the drum. Of course, the drum served dual purposes—one for the dominant White enslavers; the other for the enslaved humans themselves. For the enslavers, the drum was an instrument to force greater productivity. Its loud sounds were meant to keep the enslaved men and women bending over their crops alert and active (Rogers, 2006). As with so much of enslaved life, however, hearing the drums sound day after day in the fields led them to begin fashioning their own music—"often so melancholy," as one White minister in 1828 wrote (Ntloedibe, 2019)—but a sound they could claim as their own.

Bringing the drum with them into the community setting for Sunday's church filled the church with the sound of this music. The music combined with their African rituals: the ring shout and unifying water baptisms. It birthed community and connection that would be woven into not only Black culture and community but all of America as well. It is easy to see how the birth of gospel, blues, and jazz, as well as their later progeny, rock and roll and hip-hop, grew from those first, deep, and resonant sounds in the fields and during those small Sunday gatherings out of sight of their White overseers and enslavers.

Such community connection, as powerful as it is today, was forged piecemeal and over generations, in small acts of innovation and improvisation that accumulated over time into the force they now have. As the data in this chapter reveal, these formerly enslaved people drew on small moments of connection and meaning making that were part of their quilted life tapestry. Done mostly out of sight from their enslavers, their actions can be seen as a fundamental part of the dual life Black people have always lived alongside their White contemporaries.

The Enslaved Origins of Double Consciousness and Code Switching

It's interesting to note an unusual process as the qualitative data on "community" was analyzed. In the first iteration, "community" seemed to have the most comments. However, upon a second analysis it became apparent that the enslaved people straddled two very different communities and made varying statements related to both the enslaved community and the enslaver's community. After recoding based on the reality of forced segregation and the power differentials between both communities, the enslaved community domain yielded the second fewest data about protective factors from the sample. However, smaller numbers do not suggest lesser meaning. The attentiveness given the all-too-powerful enslaver's community (covered in the next chapter) helps explain the later interpretations of "double-consciousness" developed by W. E. B. Du Bois (1903):

> It is a peculiar sensation, this double-consciousness, this sense of always looking at one's self through the eyes of others, of measuring one's soul by the tape of a world that looks on in amused contempt and pity. One ever feels his two-ness—an American, a Negro; two souls, two thoughts, two unreconciled strivings; two warring ideals in one dark body, whose dogged strength alone keeps it from being torn asunder. (p. 2)

Later interpretations of this social psychological dynamic focused on code switching:

> Code-switching among multicultural individuals creates a dual communication system in which people are able to maintain their identities with their in-group but can still acquire tools and gain access needed to function in larger dominant society. (Yancy, 2016)

Such psychological flexibility was borne out of necessity, not desire. As these data suggest, their origins come from the enslaved people of the 17th, 18th, and 19th centuries. As George Rawick (1972) observed on the genesis of this yawning split in human relations, two communities had to develop under the same domain: "From sunup to sundown was master's time and from sundown to sunup was the time for making black community" (pp. 11–12; see also Salisbury University, 2020). Therefore, the protective factors in this in-group community domain are defined through the enslaved people's connection to others also in bondage. This chapter will explicate the protective factors of the enslaved community, followed by an accounting of the protective factors utilized by the enslaved people in relationship to their enslavers and other free Whites of the out-group, the "master" community, explored in Chapter 5.

Importantly, we have begun to add elements of our own personal stories into this work. We do so as a way to show how so much of what was brought out of slavery—both the harshness of White supremacy and the hope and resilience of Black folks seeking and finding ways to be free—have lived on in our lives and so many other Black people found across America. It is through such knitting of the past to the present that young people and those who work with them can find new opportunities of resistance and relief, not despair.

Protective Factors

The enslaved community acted like a generalized extended kinship system in which all adults looked after all children (Blassingame, 1979; Stack, 1982). This type of assistance to one another created tolerable situations and facilitated more healthy adjustment to the conditions of enslavement. During work the enslaved people were harshly exploited, but during off time they lived for themselves and created the behavioral and institutional basis that prevented them from becoming absolute victims (Helm, 2018; Rawick, 1972).

The four protective factors identified in this domain reflect in-group (between and among the enslaved people) connections of mutual support, opportunity, pride, and norms.

Mutual Support Defined as Provision of Assistance to Other Enslaved People

Bill Heard from Georgia states how it used to be in slavery times: "Times has changed in lots of ways since dem good ole days ... dey loved one another and was allus ready to lend a helpin' hand, 'specially in times of trouble."[1]

Support amongst the enslaved population was so essential that many times the configuration of the quarters made it easy to access one another. On the plantation the enslaved people usually had a house of their own for their families. "Usually they built their houses in a circle so you didn't have to go out doors hardly to go to the house next to you," says Clayton Holbert from Kansas.[2]

While many enslaved men and women made attempts to run away from bondage, Jim Taylor from Maryland also talked about the help of strangers that made his escape possible: "After arriving in Philadelphia (as escaped runaways) we went to a colored church that helped escaping slaves."[3]

Delicia Patterson from Missouri echoed that sentiment, noting that such support came from enslaved people along her route to freedom: "I run away. I stayed two weeks. I hid in the woods that whole two weeks and was not afraid. At night I would come up to some of the slave cabins who were my friends and eat and stay all night."[4]

Sometimes the support took the form of lifting spirits and having fun out of sight of the enslavers. Nancy Jackson of Texas says, "Massa gone ... and us niggers give a big ball the night they all gone."[5]

They didn't just have hidden social support; concrete support was meted out as well. Families pooled resources when they needed to go find food for each family. James Bolton of Georgia says, "Nigger mens and boys 'ud go in crowds and a rabbit ain't got no chance 'ginst that!"[6]

Certain support went beyond the enslaved family unit and impacted the entire enslaved community. The enslaved community helped one another during bereavement: "Dere warn't no undertakers back in dem days, and folks had to pervide evvything at home. Corpses was measured and coffins made to fit de bodies. All de neighbors, fur and nigh, gathered 'round to set up wid de fambly," says Bill Heard of Georgia.[7]

Clayton Holbert from Kansas says, "There wasn't such a thing as a cemetery then, they were just buried right on the plantation, usually close to the house. They would put the body in a wagon, and walk to where to bury the person, and they would sing all of the way."[8] The enslaved community also looked after the aged and elderly in their in-group community. Holbert also says, "When a slave got too old to work master would give him a small cabin on the plantation and the other slaves would wait on him, they would furnish him with victuals and clothes until he died."[9] "Besides having to take care of young children, these older slaves were required to care for those who were ill," says Henry Wright from Georgia.[10]

Barbara's Personal Experience with Community Support

When I was about 13 years old my grandmother's house caught fire on the Fourth of July, and she and my aunts and uncles were displaced for about 2 months. My grandmother was very poor, and everything she possessed was in that house. The house suffered from smoke damage and water damage. Yet what happened next stayed with me for all my life. Neighbors from my grandmother's street and others from the rest of the community all pitched in to help my grandmother and her family.

At that time my mother had recently moved into a larger home from the government housing where we had lived for the past 4 years. Red Cross offered some very temporary assistance, including some McDonald's food and red blankets and cots that allowed my displaced family members to sleep throughout our home. But what strangers did, their acts of kindness through mutual aid in the form of food, prayers, and modest provisions, helped so much by lifting our spirits that we were not alone—just the way our enslaved ancestors on the run felt 150 years ago.

Deborah's Personal Experience with Community Support

When Hurricane Sandy hit our beach community of Far Rockaway, Queens, the forces of wind and water were so severe that boats swam in the streets and sand could be found in door wells of 20-story apartment buildings. Whether well-to-do, middle class, or poor, everyone was without power, water, and food—and there was little transportation in or out. Luckily, the school our granddaughters attended across the borough (and thus away from the catastrophe) pitched in immediately. Equally important, just as in Georgia, neighbors helped neighbors. Diapers and water were shared, people helped with childcare, cans of food were swapped—it was the same kind of care and mutual aid enslaved people provided each other out of the sight of their enslavers, that flourished in the Rockaways for weeks and even months to come.

Enslaved Person Narrative Excerpt

James Bolton, 85 years old, did yard and light work in Oglethorpe County near Lexington on a plantation with over 900 acres. His entire family had "belonged" to Marse Whitfield Bolton. Once a week they would go to the big house "to git the 'lowance or vittles." They never had enough food. "They were not permitted to hunt, they had no guns and no dogs." But the enslaved community banded together for the purpose of getting more food to eat. Families pooled resources when they needed to go find food for the family. Possum and rabbit were plentiful at night on the plantation and surrounding areas. Mr. Bolton said, "Nigger mens and boys 'ud go in crowds and a rabbit ain't got no chance 'ginst that!" And when they couldn't run them down in darkness, they all got "right smart about kechin' in traps."[11]

Barbara's Client Example After Hurricane Sandy

Ashley and her family were adversely impacted in the fall of 2012 when Hurricane Sandy caused flooding in a section of their neighborhood. Their home sustained water damage in the basement where electronic equipment, books, and other items were ruined. The loss of electricity meant that food went bad too. The family had very little money to make up the shortfall for food and other necessary items. This stressed the family out. The State of New Jersey made funds available for families who didn't have health insurance to receive temporary counseling related to the trauma of the impact of the storm.

One of the inventories that was conducted at the assessment phase with the family was to identify social support from their "kiss-and-kin" network. The family was able to identify relatives and neighbors who were unaffected to the same degree by the storm and were able to connect to them for support. They were able to get access to money, food, clothing, a TV, furniture, and other donated items. A local branch of a civil rights organization also provided food and clothing to the family. Not unlike Mr. Bolton, the family often remarked how blessed they felt that people banded together to help them during their hard times. A culture of reciprocity and support, begun under bondage, continues to flourish throughout Black America. Such support, developed over centuries, is a multigenerational strength to be celebrated by old and young alike—especially if they know of its origins.

Opportunity Defined as Chance for Progress, Advancement, or Community Time Together

Harvest time meant brutally long hours of shucking, picking or stirring, as in the case of sugar on the sugar plantations of the Deep South, followed by big festivals on the plantation. These were family and community celebrations. Festivals and harvest celebrations created chances for the enslaved people to connect with each other at sundown and on weekends. Tom Hawkins of Georgia looked forward to the weekends; he said, "Sadday nights dey all got together and frolicked; picked de banjo, and drunk whiskey. Didn't none of 'em git drunk, 'cause dey was used to it."[12] Clayton Holbert from Kansas says, "The slaves used to dance or go to the prayer meeting to pass their time."[13]

When the enslaved people got together it provided opportunities for sharing information about the plantation, neighboring plantations, local figures, politics, and more. Doc Daniel Dowdy from Oklahoma tells of the enslaved people's information grapevine: "They carried news from one plantation by what they call relay."[14] The same kind of exchange happened mostly during gatherings for women. Camilla Jackson from Georgia talks about a community quilting project:

> "One of the most enjoyable affairs in those days was the quilting party. Every night they would assemble at some particular house and help that person to finish her quilts. The next night, a visit would be made to some one else's home and so on, until everyone had a sufficient amount of bed-clothing made for the winter. Besides this was an excellent chance to get together for a pleasant time and discuss the latest gossip."[15]

Dan Bogie from Kentucky says, "We did not work on Saturday afternoon. The men would go fishing and the women would go to the neighbors and help each other piece quilts."[16]

Barbara's Personal Experience with Opportunity

When I was growing up we used to have a regular block party in the summertime. This was a chance for all the folks in the neighborhood to come together and share potluck meals and barbecue, listen to music and dance, and play games. It was really a time for just enjoying life with our neighbors. Sometimes we had T-shirts made and sold for the food and such, but it also seemed to help us all bond ourselves as members of the same Camden, New Jersey, community.

The church also featured very prominently in our community as a place for connection with one another. It's where we got news from the preacher about other families. The church was where we dressed up in our finest clothes and made common commitment to serve the Lord and to love and help one another. It's where we prayed together. After the service there was always a huge feast: food and desserts combined with lots of chitchatting between the congregants. It was a time when prayers were answered in the form of receiving an envelope with some money in it because one of the church ladies found out that somebody lost their job or had some hardship. Or you heard people sharing information about job leads for those looking for work. People would talk about their homes or their yard work and who was helping who do what in their houses. Folks passed along names of people in the neighborhood who could help with that rotten tree in the backyard, that dent in the car fender, a paint job, or extermination of bugs. Mutual aid was just what people did for each other, passing one helping hand to another.

Deborah's Personal Experience with Opportunity

I have spent a lifetime believing in the value of education on a number of levels. First, in this country education may not be equitable and may be part of the privilege of the wealthy, but it is attainable even if it must be self-directed. Education, once attained, cannot be taken away. It is yours to keep, to wear proudly, and to even allow to manifest and blossom into lifelong smile-bearing learning. Graduations are as much of a favorite celebration of mine today as they were growing up. Graduation is that visible commodity, proudly shouting, "I earned this, and I have paperwork to prove that I have been ordained smart!"

There is, of course, the sharing in this celebration of acquired knowledge. This celebration may be through a lens of gratitude simply because you held strong doubts that you could make it this far, or through a lens of having no more tuition bills pile up, or a lens of representing your family's potential, as you took one more step than they did, brandishing pride and hope for more opportunity and the solid footing to make it.

My memories of my great-grandmother are thinly veiled in a young girl's vision of family values and tradition. She was a woman of few words but spoken so you would have no doubt about what she said. She would proudly tell you that she was born when Lincoln was president. I never saw how tall she stood, nor was I ever privy to why she used a wheelchair. But I did know of her seriousness. On one of our family visits from New York to Atlantic City, I overheard my grandmother mentioning in passing and simply as a matter of fact that my great-grandmother owned a small business but that through the normal happenings for Black people in the post-Reconstruction South some White folks did not believe a woman of color should own a business. It was simply taken away from her.

I believe that my grandmother became an elementary school teacher because she could empower her children as well as others without her education being taken away from her. She began with my mom. With whatever resources she had, she invested in my mother's education; she made sure that my mother had the opportunity to complete her undergraduate degree. I have often wondered where my admiration for education and learning stem from; well that's easy enough to decipher. If our granddaughter does what she says she will do, she will, become a fifth-generation Black American teacher in this country, with the ultimate legacy of her great-grandmother, one of the first Black principals in Westchester County, a legacy well described by Bill Withers (1971):

> Grandma's hands
> Soothed an unwed mother
> Grandma's hands
> Used to ache sometimes and swell

Enslaved Person Narrative Excerpt

Camilla Jackson, 80 years old, worked the fields on a plantation in Georgia owned by Dr. Peter Hoyle. All of the enslaved people, male and female, were required to work the fields. She did so until she was 12 years old and then was given a job in the house. She operated a fly brush to keep the flies out of the house. Her enslaver permitted them to visit other plantations after work hours, if the other enslaver agreed with that level of "free" travel.

When the enslaved people got together it provided opportunities for sharing information about the plantation, neighboring plantations, local figures, politics, and more. Mrs. Jackson recollected about a community quilting project:

> "One of the most enjoyable affairs in those days was the quilting party. Every night they would assemble at some particular house and help that person to finish her quilts. The next night, a visit would be made to some one else's home and so on, until everyone had a sufficient amount of bed-clothing made for the winter. Besides this was an excellent chance to get together for a pleasant time and discuss the latest gossip."

How alike this example is of life in a poor Camden, New Jersey, neighborhood 100 years later!

Barbara's Client Example

The Stewart family moved into the New York metropolitan area from North Carolina and felt socially isolated. The mom felt like there were more employment opportunities in the North. Dinesha, 14 years old, missed her friends from the old neighborhood and her school. At the time I was providing therapy services for students who were struggling with adjustment disorders related to transitioning from middle school to high school. Dinesha had difficulty concentrating and getting to school on time and was withdrawing and isolating. The move was hard on her.

Dinesha's family was unfamiliar with their new city. They wanted to make connections with other African American families and begin building their community. In North Carolina they had a vibrant community where the church was the center of their life. They were interested in finding a local Baptist church that had a choir and youth program.

They were encouraged to attend the school's parent support meetings, a multifamily psychoeducational and support program to meet other parents who could give them information about churches and other programs and services in the community. The family began attending meetings, building connection to other families with more history in their new community, and getting reliable information and even offers to attend church with a couple of other parents. The family "shopped" around for a Baptist church in the city and became regular attendees.

Dinesha and her mom joined the choir as well as other service boards at the church over the next 6 months. Dinesha's mood and behaviors improved as she deepened connection to the youth ministry, developed new relationships with peers, and began to do service in the community. She was in the culinary tract at her high school and liked the food pantry ministry at the church. Her grades and attendance improved, and her overall adjustment was positive to the new school and community. Like Mrs. Jackson, Dinesha also found support, companionship and an outlet for her creativity in a quilting group.

Deborah's Educational Example

When charter schools first started to come into being in the NYC metropolitan area, they had a bit of leeway in how curricula would be delivered, the length of the school day, and what resources would be used to augment the dictates of traditional education. People of color leapt at the opportunity to attend a school that might embrace their cultural heritage as a contribution and not as an appendage that could be removed or shifted at will. In one such instance, a charter school in its infancy managing grades K–2 (charter schools would grow a grade per year) found they had a portion of students (mostly students of color) who would benefit from additional resources. Administrators and teachers soon became aware that the portion of students needing more services was large enough that it could not be ignored, for to do so would potentially sentence many of them to diminished levels of literacy and a lack of growth in overall learning.

Therefore, an enrichment program was designed so that any student who needed help would receive it in ways that met their individual learning style. The program was designed by the teachers and was offered on Saturday mornings. There was only one requisite for participation and that was that at least one of the parents must be present. As the child learned, the parent learned the child's educational needs in real time with the same instructors who taught their children each school day. As time went on and as parents continued to attend, they understood not only the learning styles of their children but also of the children sitting with them. A kind of communal learning practice was generated, with parents supporting each other and all of their children. As with the enslaved women's Sunday quilting bees, sharing information deepened the bond of connection and the children's opportunities to advance in their learning.

Pride Defined as Awareness and Celebration of Shared Cultural History

The creation of patterns of family and community life that were functionally integrative for enslaved people did more than merely prevent the destruction of personality that often occurs when individuals struggle to attain the unattainable. It was part and parcel of the social process out of which came Black pride, Black identity, Black culture, Black community, and Black rebellion in America (Dodson, 2002; Rawick, 1972).

Pride took many forms. John Barker from Texas declared with pride, "We was born slaves, malagasser niggers."[17] Maggie Woods from Arkansas says, "My folks were field hands. They was all pure African stock. All Black folks like me."[18] Willis Williams from Florida expressed the importance of reclaiming education once emancipation permitted it, stating, "soon after the smoke of the cannons had died down and people began thinking of the future, the Negroes turned their thoughts toward education. They grasped every opportunity to learn to read and write."[19] Clairborne Moss from Arkansas spoke on the power of the community when banded together: "The Ku Klux kept the niggers scared. They cowed them down so that they wouldn't go to the polls. ... But they couldn't keep the niggers in Hancock County away from the polls. There was too many of us."[20] Willie Ann Smith from Texas spoke about the common yearning to be free: "We slips off and have prayer but daren't 'low the white folks to know it and sometimes we hums 'ligious songs low like when we's workin'. It was our way of prayin' to be free, but the white folks didn't know it."[21]

Fannie Berry of Virigina says, "My master told us dat de niggers started the railroad, an' dat a nigger lookin' at a boilin' coffee pot on a stove one day got the idea dat he could cause it to run by putting wheels on it. Dis nigger being a blacksmith put his thoughs into action by makin' wheels an' put coffee on it, an' by some kinder means he made it run an' the idea wuz stole from him an' dey built de steam engine."[22]

Martin Jackson from Texas said the following:

> "The master's name was usually adopted by a slave after he was set free. This was done more because it was the logical thing to do and the easiest way to be identified than it was through affection for the master. Also, the government seemed to be in a almighty hurry to have us get names. We had to register as someone, so we could be citizens. Well, I got to thinkin about all us slaves that was going to take the name Fitzpatrick. I made up my mind I'd find me a different one. One of my grandfathers in Africa was called Jeaceo, and so I decided to be Jackson."[23]

Multigenerational legacies took so many forms!

Barbara's Personal Experience with Pride

At 9 years old I moved into the government housing with my mother. She was 23. The government housing were brand new. My mother immediately started to grow flowers in the grass in the front and backyards. She felt very accomplished as a teenage, recently single mother having her own home. Against all the odds, she had become a homeowner.

When I grew in Camden 50 years ago, it was conventional wisdom that people took care of property when it was their own. And I remember some of the conversations with the other Black women in the government housing as they talked about the flowers and what it meant to them to have a home of their own. They had shared pride in beautifying their gardens.

My mother also had a picture of Black Jesus in our house, which was a radical act 50 years ago. Her mother would not stand for such a thing. My mother also taught me about the civil rights movement, and I felt both her anger and rage as much as pride in the fact that we, as Black people, as long-suffering as we were in the 1950s and 1960s, were able to come together and fight for our civil rights. She made sure we attended many community meetings at the Young Women's Christian Association around election time, learning about safety and self-defense. We got help with tutoring and we learned life-saving skills like swimming. I heard the word "empowerment" in those places. We met community leaders, people who were standing up for us and who advocated for us to have good schools, accountable politicians, recreation for children, and ambulance and fire services in our neighborhood. I learned about Kwanzaa. I learned about the Black Panthers. As with the enslaved communities of long ago, for me it was the ultimate in-group experience of resilience and growth among a people whom much of the outside world would have seen as simply poor and oppressed.

Deborah's Personal Experience with Pride

I grew up with a strong sense of self instilled in me by my mother, who was the principal of a New York elementary school located in one of the wealthiest and Whitest suburban areas of Westchester County. While attending a small, private college in Wisconsin as one of the few Black students in the college or nearby community, I was recommended by the school for the prestigious Semester at Sea program, a national "floating university" where a select few were admitted to travel and learn while at sea and at ports in Europe, Africa, and parts of Asia.

I was never quite certain how I was accepted, coming from the small Midwestern school that I did, but it was clear that the interview process helped. When asked "Why should we take you?" my response was straightforward and implicitly filled with pride: "Because you don't have me yet." Call it chutzpah or audacity, but to my mind my response came from pride in who I was and where I came from. It's part of what led me to leave the ship when warned not to while docking in apartheid South Africa and enter the Parliament building in order to register as "colored"—an audacious act that led me quickly back to the protection of the ship. If I had not been raised with a sense of self in my own community, reinforced within my family, such confidence would have evaporated long before that interview or the later strong arm of the law that literally grabbed my arm and forced me back to the ship's safe haven. Whatever bruise they left on my shoulder couldn't diminish the sense of empowerment I felt—just as the enslaved woman from Missouri must have felt during her 2 weeks of freedom.

Enslaved Person Narrative Excerpt

The activity of the the enslaved in creating patterns of family and community life that were functionally integrative did more than merely prevent the destruction of personality that often occurs when individuals struggle unsuccessfully to attain the unattainable. It was part and parcel of the social process out of building resilient communities. It began with pride in their Blackness.

John Barker, age 84, worked the fields on a Texas plantation and exclaimed in his first sentence to the WPA agent taking down his story of bondage, "I was born a slave. I am a Malagasser (Madagascar) nigger."[24] For Maggie Woods, age 70, her folks were all field hands with Marse Douglas in Arkansas. She began her interview and said, "My folks was all pure African stock. All Black folks like me." Her story relays the survival story of her family after the war. And she concluded the interview by stating, "I lived on what I am able to work and make. I never got no help from the government." Her self-reliance was a source of pride and, for both Mr. Barker and herself, communicated their Black identity and connection to the African homeland.

Barbara's Client Example

The Black community in which my private practice was located was anchored by several civil rights organizations who routinely held cultural events. One of the largest events each year is the Kwanzaa celebration. Kwanzaa was created by Dr. Maulana Karenga and was first observed in 1966–1967 at the height of the Black Power movement and Pan-Africanism in urban America. It is a celebration observed from December 26th to January 1st and ends in gift-giving and a feast. The core principals (Nguzo Saba) are as follows:

- *Umoja* (unity): To strive for and to maintain unity in the family, community, nation, and race.
- *Kujichagulia* (self-determination): To define and name ourselves, as well as to create and speak for ourselves.
- *Ujima* (collective work and responsibility): To build and maintain our community together and make our brothers' and sisters' problems our problems and to solve them together.
- *Ujamaa* (cooperative economics): To build and maintain our own stores, shops, and other businesses and to profit from them together.

- *Nia* (purpose): To make our collective vocation the building and developing of our community in order to restore our people to their traditional greatness.
- *Kuumba* (creativity): To always do as much as we can, in the way we can, in order to leave our community more beautiful and beneficial than we inherited it.
- *Imani* (faith): To believe with all our hearts in our people, our parents, our teachers, our leaders, and the righteousness and victory of our struggle.

These core principles are meant to illustrate culturally rooted values to sustain connection and pride of African Americans long separated from the motherland. It is obvious in the enslaved people narratives that the commitment to pride, mutual support, and connection that Kwaanzaa embodies began long ago among an enslaved people who still found a way to create a community of connection between their families and those who lived in close proximity to them.

Deborah's Educational Example

There is no question that the church has and continues to be an integral weaving through many facets of the Black American experience. It is a matter of inherited pride and respect, so much so that when a set of Black twins were sent to a Catholic school, it was a merging of pride, faith, and the pursuit of an education all in one sweet package. And this was fine for some time; the twins were completely immersed in the traditional rituals and milestones that define the Catholic faith. Their academic achievements were comparable to their devotion to their faith. They felt wholly included in all things and wanted to express their pride; they mentioned to the presiding nuns that their aunts were nuns.

The response was an immediate schism in how the twins were treated and approached. Where they once held the privilege of having starring or significant roles in the school plays, they were now assigned menial tasks by a number of the sisters. They were not called on to participate in class discussions. There was every reason for them to give up. However, with their mother's help and guidance they learned to distinguish between those nuns who were now hostile and those who remained supportive, even if done so quietly. Rather than leave the school, they focused their studies as much as possible under the tutelage of those who embraced their talents. Not unlike the enslaved members who knew how to discern less hostile enslavers and their wives from truly vicious ones (which we discuss in the next chapter), the twins not only graduated from this school but also did well enough to go on to college.

Norms Defined as Behaviors that Preserve, Protect and Strengthen the Enslaved Community and Its Members

It was critical for the enslaved to understand the spoken and unspoken rules of the plantation and the ways of the White enslavers. Such knowledge could be the difference between life and death, or between eating supper or getting a whipping. For example, there were penalties if the enslaver heard you praying at night. "Durin' slavery de slaves hadder keep quiet en dey would turn a kittle upside down ter keep de white folks 'yearin dere prayers en chants, says Ellis Ken Kannon from Tennessee."[25]

Tom Hawkins from Georgia describes the rigid behavioral expectation of the community while securing nourishment for the families: "Under a long shed built next to de kitchen was a long trough. At night dey (marster and missus) crumbled cornbread in it and poured it full of buttermilk. Grown folks and chilluns all gathered 'roun' dat old trough and et out of it wid deir wooden spoons. ... Dere warn't no fightin' 'roun' dat trough. Dey all knowed better'n dat."[26]

Fannie Griffin from South Carolina recalls the following difficult lesson she learned the hard way: "I 'members one time I slip off from de missus and go to a dance and when I come back, de dog in de yard didn't seem to know me and he bark and wake de missus up and she whip me something awful. I sho didn't go to no more dances widout asking her."[27] Another South Carolinian, Alexander Scaife, reported a similar experience: "We made good corn liquor. Once a week I bring a gallon to de big house to Marster. Once I got happy off'n it, and when I got don lots of it was gone. He had me whipped. Dat de last time I ever got happy off'n Martster's jug."[28]

Many of the enslaved people recount holidays, such as Christmas and harvest times, as times when they were treated to special goodies from the enslaver, but there were rules. James Lucas from Mississippi remembers that "slaves received a heap 'o fresh meat an' whiskey for treats. But you better not git drunk. No-sir-ree!!" [29]

Another guarded behavioral expectation was related to protection when leaving the plantation grounds (this does not include running away). Lucy Mccullough from Georgia said, "Us wuz mo' skeered er patter-rollers den any thing else. Patter-rollers diden' bodder folks much, lessen dey caught 'em offen dar marsters plantations en dey diden hab no pass."[30] Tom Hawkins from Georgia says, "Us alus had to have a pass if us left de plantation for anthing or de patterollers was apt to git ou and look out den, for you was sho' to git a larrupin' in dey cotch you off 'f'um home widout no pass."[31]

These rigid rules extended to basic communication. Bert Mayfield from Kentucky talks about the importance of maintaining the boundaries of communication in mixed company: "The negroes would talk among themselves, but never carried talks to the white folks."[32] To do so was to invite trouble into the home and community. As one can see, code switching was created generations before the term itself was recognized.

Henry Wright from Georgia also expresses value in spiritual matters despite the risk: "Although slaves prayed for their freedom they were afraid to even sing any type of spiritual for fear of being punished."[33] And lastly, Reverend Squires Jackson of Florida put the other protective factors in perspective in that modifications in behavior were in the interest of moving the community toward freedom: "It is interesting to know that slaves on this plantation were not allowed to sing when they were at work, but with all the vigilance of the overseers, nothing could stop those silent songs of labor and prayers for freedom."[34] Deep down all of the enslaved people knew that their norm was to be free as much as anyone else—even if they did so, under bondage, through out-of-sight rituals and quiet hymns.

Barbara's Personal Experience with Norms and Values

I had a curfew when I was a teenager. It was 8:00 p.m. Missing curfew meant a severe punishment. My friends know about it, and for the most part, it was no problem. But one time I was hanging out at a friend's house who lived about two blocks away from my home. When I noticed the time it was 7:57 p.m. I jumped up out of that sofa and ran out of Alice's front door on to Elm Street and made a right-hand turn heading toward Eighth Street. At the corner I made a right-hand turn, went half a block to Birch Street, and made a left on Birch, running as fast as I could to 835 Birch Street. Along the way, a few people sitting on porches, who were my mothers and grandmothers, shouted comments to me as I ran on: "You better be running! You know if you're not there by 8:00, your mom's going to whoop your behind!" How on Earth did they know that? At that time the community looked out for each other; parents and neighbors talked to each other. They made explicit agreements with one another to look after each other. My mom did the same when we were out and about the community and she ran into a child who she thought was out of place or up to something suspicious, and she would say something like, "What you doing out here? Does your mom know you are over here?" And of course that young person knew in that moment that if their mother didn't know, she sure would know soon, because my mother would tell them. Lessons of connection demanding safety and strict adherence to keeping them clear and delineated did not show up in Camden in the 1960s and 1970s. They began on those slave plantations centuries ago as a way to survive and, whenever possible, away from their White overseers, thrive.

There was also value in respecting elders, and I still adhere to that. Rarely will you hear me not address an obvious elder as "mister" or "missus." And you would be hard-pressed to ever hear me say a curse word in front of them. My mother heard me say the word "damn" once when I was in my 30s, and she shot me a look that was like shooting a bullet. I knew better. We didn't talk back to grown-ups. Elders were respected during the time of slavery as a norm that strengthened the entire community that lived on in the 1960s. Framed correctly today through an understanding of the past, perhaps we can re-create it in the 21st century.

Education was also a value, as was the importance of a strong work ethic. For me it was an expectation that I would get educated, given that my mother sacrificed so much to make certain that happened. Given our poverty, there could be no financial inheritance. My mother, instead, like Maggie Woods and so many other enslaved people a century earlier, felt she had done her job by providing me with the means to be educated so that I could go on to make a better life for myself than she had.

Deborah's Personal Experience with Norms and Values

There was a time when at least one family member was home to make sure none of the children in our household would be latch-key kids. There was always someone who would watch out for us until we were mature enough to watch out for ourselves. When economic conditions continued to whittle resources and significantly downsize quality of life from what was already a hair away from poverty, both parents had to work. While my family was not as poor as some, communities valued protecting all its children, including mine. There was a kind of communal parenting, where neighborhood parents, often working different shifts, would act as guardians and keep an eye out for the safety and security of the neighborhood children.

Mrs. Collins, a proud older woman of color, would watch the children as we left for school and knew the schedules of when we were to return home. She wanted to make sure they managed to soak up as much education as possible because for her it was more than a simple guarantee of educational attainment; for her, it was also the guarantee that once there you could continue layering all that information—and, as she said, "No one could take it away from you."

One day Mrs. Collins spotted my brother Aaron on the streets in the middle of the day. She approached him and asked him why he wasn't in school. He replied that he was sick. And without wasting another breath, she asked him, "So why are you outside? If you're sick, go home." He turned and went back home. She had evidence that he did in fact go home, as she asked our mother, who mentioned that she talked to him on the phone, which was shortly after Mrs. Collins confronted him. Lessons learned from enslaved people on the need for community vigilance in support of each other lived on in Mrs. Collins—and in Aaron too.

Enslaved Person Narrative Excerpt

Reverend Squires Jackson, 96 years old and from Florida, put the other protective factors in perspective when he stated that modifications in behavior were in the interest of moving the community toward freedom: "It is interesting to know that slaves on this plantation were not allowed to sing when they were at work, but with all the vigilance of the overseers, nothing could stop those silent songs of labor and prayers for freedom." Deep down all enslaved people knew that the norm was to be free and to stay alive. Embedded in this wise quotation is a deep resilience and commitment to those with whom one lived within the enslaved community that lives on in Black communities today.

Barbara's Client Example

Ms. Arnold, Shaquan's mother, was very anxious that the fate of Trayvon Martin, the Sanford, Florida, teen stalked and killed by George Zimmerman in February of 2012, would be the fate of her 17-year-old son. She and other mothers raised the issue of how to protect their African American sons from racial profiling and violence at the hands of police or others during a parent support group with four other African American parents. The mothers generated a list of behaviors and attitudes that they believed would help protect their teenage children if they were to encounter the police. They developed agreements within the group to talk to their children about cooperation, modulating the tones of their voices, showing their hands, and being respectful in the event that they encountered police or other authority figures like teachers. The parents also emphasized the need to get out of the dangerous police encounter as the goal and to get home and to relay the experience to their parents so that parents can then decide the next steps. Many affirmed that they would join organizations in the community that were working on police reform. Several community organizations sprung up to meet the need for the community. Shaquan and his mom joined in several protest marches in the community and rallies at the steps of the city hall. Shaquan was fired up about the issue and wrote several rap songs to inspire other peers to join in and to make smart choices in the moment of a police encounter. While I was engaged with this family, there was no report of any actual police encounter with Shaquan or his mother. I felt that they had rehearsed and prepared for the possibility in every way possible. They both took on leadership and became advocates for other children, helping give their teens specific ways to avoid worsening the situation. During family support meetings Shaquan and his mom also spoke about the need to pray as well as encourage and teach their children new skills and attitudes. Their leadership in forging community connection and safety for young Black youth kept Shaquan and others safe from harm in the years ahead.

Implications for Today: The Binds That Didn't Break

Black folks figured out ways to survive when out of sight of their White overlords. They could have moments of happiness, even when their communities were thought to be nonexistent. Black folks figured out ways to connect to one another, carrying on West African traditions and values of member-to-member support no matter what the enslaver threw at their Black families. No enslaver's lash was long enough to throttle Black families from surviving and their communities from being built.

"Community" is suggestive of mutual aid and bonds that tie people together. Look how difficult it was to engage in behaviors so fundamentally human—singing, supporting, providing—in short, to connect. These narratives are filled with stories of people who went to any length to build community, to create new rituals, to support each other—in short, to help each other survive.

The narratives make it clear that there is a duality of the lived experience for every enslaved person on the plantation, where they first must learn to navigate living in subjugation under the closer scrutiny of the White man by day and then somehow live in their Black skin in relation to other Black people in the community from sundown to sunup.

Dual Consciousness Lives On: Our Personal Stories

We know what it is like as Black women in America. Even in 2021, frequently we are the only "ones" in the midst of White people in our places of employment. In these jobs we must look a certain way, rest a certain way, eat a certain way. There are expectations about our temperament being a certain way in mixed company. This is something our mothers taught us when we were little girls about how to act right when around White people. We had to be clean and we had to "represent the race." There was an expectation that we would be courteous and respectful, but if someone calls us the "n" word we were to stand up to them, and then we were supposed to tell mama, who would straighten it out. As professionals, we have heard a similar refrain so often from so many of our Black clients. Our Black children have been told not to wear cornrows or not to wear certain clothing and, above all, never to raise their voice to authority. As teenagers and young adults, we did not dare make eye contact directly with someone in authority. There were so many codes and duties to perform to get through the day and avoid "trouble."

It was different when around our own people. All of a sudden the dialect changed, a sense of relaxation enveloped us, and we knew we were amongst people who meant us no harm. People didn't care what clothing we had on except for Sundays in church. The use of language changes when we are around our people. No one is afraid of somebody talking too fast or raising their voice or cussing a little bit or running the dozens on you. We are home and are safe to be who we are.

Our work makes clear that is the way enslaved men and women felt from sundown to sunup. No one would've denied any enslaved person the need to just find a place in the quarters to lay their head and to rest after a day of backbreaking work in service to the oppressor in preparation for the next day's work. But there's something restorative about just being with your family and your people. It's good for the soul. As these narratives make clear, Black folks are used to creating dual lives. A survival strategy forged in bondage lives on as psychic strain and unresolved trauma in 21st-century Black communities—unless and until we forge ways so that each of us are able to live fully as one person, no longer trapped between two worlds.

Often, to the outsider—and perhaps even to some White historians who have told the story of Black families in slavery—the superficial appearance of how Black people lived in their quarters away from their enslavers may create the illusion of joviality among the enslaved, even while under bondage. As the narratives make clear, there was joy in the midst of the unyielding pain of bondage; it was the joy of survival. It was the joy of knowing that even though the oppressor made life hell, you beat them at their own game. It was in this hidden experience from White enslavers that our families and our communities were maintained—experiences still hidden from most of White America in the 21st century.

As the narratives in each chapter suggest, the totality of what we've experienced has become one of the great paradoxes of American life: during enslavement, Black folks lived under repression of expression and active limitation of living a full human life. Yet the result of these constraints, begun in those mournful sounds in the fields long ago, was the creation of music, movement, sound, and language that have emerged as central parts of the defining characteristics of what it means to be an "American." Even under the enslaver's lash, we developed our music, our clothing, our dialect, our dancing, and our mannerisms that have been emulated, appropriated, and respected throughout the last 100-plus years by dominant White culture. Whether jazz or hip-hop music, hoping to be cool, high-fiving, or learning the lindy, the stroll, or swing, Black culture, born of evident pain and hidden hope, has contributed mightily to all of America—even as some people never even noticed.

Hope is in the midst of heartache in these narratives that have been presented as a set of powerful lessons of possibility for young people. Otherwise, given the police murders of so many Black men and women and the universal need for parents to have "the talk" with their children at younger and younger ages, what prevents youth from breaking psychologically when the odds seem to be so stacked against them? How far does one go before losing oneself? What we know is that we want to be fully integrated people, able to live without dual consciousness and double lives that rob us of the opportunity to be people fully integrated into the richly diverse society known as America.

Like John Barker and Maggie Woods from 100 years ago, what sustains us and gives us hope is when we have seen young people, despite the odds, succeeding at adapting to political and environmental circumstances in ways that give purpose to their lives. When this happens, they know what it means to state, "We are still here." Our resilience comes shining through, in large part because of consciously making use of protective factors that have been passed on to us from our ancestors. We know we must support one another in the Black community and that we cannot afford to be in fierce competition with one another when we're all suffering at the hands of the oppressor. Helping to create opportunity for one another is part of the survival plan. Our connection to one another and to our shared culture fosters a sense of pride and establishes clear norms and values for all members of the community. It is for these reasons we continue to have victory in the face of oppression.

And Yet, Hidden Scars Remain

But, as DeGruy-Leary (2005) makes clear, not one Black person is unscathed from the deleterious effects of sustained oppression. As Black professionals who have worked for decades within our communities, we also know there is a certain amount of learned helplessness and internalized self-hatred expressed by some Black folks. The relentless, pervasive barrage of messaging that tells us how little Black lives are worth impacts us.

Perhaps there isn't that communal supervision of our youth like there used to be when we were was growing up in the 1960s and 1970s. But notice how many of the formerly enslaved people were saying the same thing about young people and the lack of everyone pitching in for them almost a hundred years ago! As each of our families used to say, what goes around comes around. If either of us was up to no good, eventually our mamas would find out. Perhaps that's still something we need to seek out today—in our churches, mosques, schools, community centers, and homes.

The Sankofa Guidance for Practitioners and Educators: Working with the Black Community

1. Work for justice. The implication for practice on this level is in seeking for ways to remedy long-standing problems in the Black community. This goal can be acted on and supported by social workers educating, agitating, and organizing for change. The lesson from the enslaved person narratives is to rebel and resist and to struggle for justice, even in small, incremental ways to experience a taste of freedom and agency (Rawick, 1972). Social workers can participate in formal and informal mechanisms to achieve social justice on behalf of their clients. Social workers can also connect youth and families to important and relevant causes impacting their lives and communities (Schiele, 1996).

2. Connect Black youth to leaders. Key in this domain is the need to identify formal and informal community leadership and to connect our youth to those leaders, whether they be a church deacon who during the week works for sanitation, a hairdresser known for extensions, or Aunt Millie who bakes those cakes every Saturday afternoon.

3. Pass the torch of leadership to Black youth. This also means beginning to develop the leadership skills of Black youth so that they can make a difference in their own communities. It is critical for established leaders in the Black community to turn their attention to developing the next generation of leadership for the community. Bernice Johnson Reagon (1988) of Sweet Honey in the Rock composed "Ella's Song," which captures this imperative in its lyrics:

Passing on to others that which was passed on to me

... Young people come first, they have the courage where we fail

4. Mentor Black youth. Our job as community elders is to reach back to youth and teach them how to sustain our movement for social justice. We need to create apprenticeships, internships, fellowships, and shadowing opportunities in our civic and community organizations. We can invest in their education by sending them to organizing and leadership academies, such as the Midwest Academy, boot camps for leadership, or university leadership academies for girls and disadvantaged youth. Those opportunities exist in both our own communities as well as the larger community; we need to take the time to connect young people to these resources.
5. Support Black youth entrepreneurship. It is important to support Black businesses and Black entrepreneurship. Many young people we know have brilliant business ideas, are innovative, and are natural hustlers. With guidance, mentoring, and training they can parlay those skills into some self-reliance and pride. I, Barbara, had a client who was very good at repairing bicycles. He could take one apart and put it back together with his eyes closed. In sessions he would frequently express sadness about not having enough money to do the things he liked to do, such as going to the movies, taking the train into New York City to walk around, or buying food and clothing that he wanted. When I did an assessment of his strengths and discovered this passion and acuity for bicycle repair, we launched the idea of marketing his skills and services to others so that he could earn a stream of income. He created flyers. He distributed the flyers in his community and around the school. He did house calls, and kids could take their bikes to him. He became skilled at finding spare parts for cheap and creating inventory for himself. I watched him generalize his hustle and natural talent into a successful seasonal business venture.

6. Connect Black youth to Black elders. We have to connect Black youth to Black elders. Black elders hold the history of our communities and of our people. We've often observed the pattern of generational teenage motherhood: Many 15-year-old clients had a 30-year-old mother, a 45-year-old grandmother, and a 60-year-old great-grandmother. And what we've observed so often is that Black youth do not connect to the lived experience of the great-grandmothers and great-grandfathers in their midst.

On the other hand, the child welfare system oftentimes forces engagement of our elderly into primary parenting roles with Black children when their biological parents, for a variety of reasons, cannot safely and properly raise their children. The system as currently constituted places biological grandchildren in the care of their grandparents without sufficient financial and other support such as non-biological foster parents would receive. This perverts the idea of connecting to the wisdom of our elders, as elders are then cast into highly stressful, time-consuming primary caregiver roles at times in their lives where they may be experiencing other maladies of older age, caring for their own spouses, and, if in retirement, already experiencing the financial pinches of leaving the workforce. We have to do better by our elders in the Black community specifically and for all seniors generally in America. By most measures, we fail our elderly, and we must do better.

7. Acceptance of LGBTQIA+ Black youth prevents death. This is an important point to raise for the LGBTQIA+ youth and adults in our community. As the enslaved person narratives make clear, it goes against the values and norms of our culture to reject a family member. We place the highest value on interdependence and connection to one another. Rejection of our children, teenagers, and adults who are seeking to be their authentic gendered and sexual selves runs counter to the values and does catastrophic harm to the individual, family, and community. Research is clear about consequences of rejection of LGBTQIA+ youth by the community. All too often, that rejection leads to severe mental illness and in many cases suicide and death (Ryan, 2010).

I (Barbara) am a second-generation lesbian who was rejected by my lesbian mother, who was rejected by her family, all under the guise of religion. In my view this is a perversion of religion. I cannot overstate the importance of love, tolerance and acceptance of diversity within the Black community or the damage done by excluding and shaming some members, especially young people. It is better to struggle around these hard issues by keeping your teen close and the lines of communication open. Just as our enslaved ancestors did each day of their lives, it is better to struggle around these hard issues by keeping your teen close and of out of harm's way.

8. Give back to the Black community. Far too many Black folks make it out of the Black community and never return. Far too many of us have abandoned the Black community of our perhaps more impoverished youth. The Black community needs Black professionals, Black investors, and successful Black business, civic, and professional organizations. If you are on the municipal payroll as a teacher or police officer, or any other government civil service position, perhaps it would be invaluable to live in the community in which you work. We must be advocates for community development and help to get dollars into the community to build up the infrastructure to sustain our families and our youth.

9. The Black community needs White investment. We are still so segregated in this country. White folks have the privilege of not necessarily needing to interact with the Black community at all. Here, White allies have choices: They can support Black businesses, Black institutions, and civic organizations. The NAACP, Black Lives Matter, and other related organizations need money and members.

Join them. Black soul-food restaurants need patrons. Book a reservation. You can invest in those businesses and financially support them. Black Lives Matters needs White allies. Sign their petition. Go to a rally. It's all your choice. What matters to you? What are you willing to do differently? How will you demonstrate that you are an ally? If you choose to support Black business, Black institutions, and Black causes, then that choice will ultimately help the Black community, Black families, and Black youth.

Endnotes

Excerpts from the Federal Writers' Project Slave Narrative (FWPSN) Collection

1. FWPSN, Georgia, Part 2, p. 138
2. FWPSN, Kansas, p. 2
3. FWPSN, Maryland, p. 64
4. FWPSN, Missouri, p. 273
5. FWPSN, Texas, Part 2, p. 194
6. FWPSN, Georgia, Part 1, p. 93
7. FWPSN, Georgia, Part 2, p. 141
8. FWPSN, Kansas, p. 3
9. FWPSN, Kansas, p. 9
10. FWPSN, Georgia, Part 4, p. 199
11. FWPSN, Georgia, Part 1, p. 93
12. FWPSN, Georgia, Part 2, p. 131
13. FWPSN, Kansas, p. 3
14. FWPSN, Oklahoma, p. 78
15. FWPSN, Georgia, Part 2, p. 296
16. FWPSN, Kentucky, p. 3
17. FWPSN, Texas, Part 1, p. 42
18. FWPSN, Arkansas, Part 7, p. 232
19. FWPSN, Florida, p. 352
20. FWPSN, Arkansas, Part 5, p. 165
21. FWPSN, Texas, Part 4, p. 43
22. FWPSN, Virginia, p. 2
23. FWPSN, Texas, Part 2, p. 192
24. FWPSN, Texas, Part 1, p. 42
25. FWPSN, Tennessee, p. 38
26. FWPSN, Georgia, Part 2, p. 128
27. FWPSN, South Carolina, Part 2, p. 210
28. FWPSN, South Carolina, Part 4, p. 76
29. FWPSN, Mississippi, p. 92
30. FWPSN, Georgia, Part 3, p. 68

31. FWPSN, Georgia, Part 2, p. 129
32. FWPSN, Kentucky, p. 16
33. FWPSN, Georgia, Part 4, p. 203
34. FWPSN, Florida, p. 178

References

Blassingame, J. W. (1979). *The slave community: Plantation life in the antebellum South.* Oxford University Press.

Burghardt, S. (2014). *Macro practice in social work for the 21st century.* Cognella Academic Publishing.

Desrochers, R., Jr. (1997). Not fade away: The narrative of Venture Smith, an African American in the early republic. *The Journal of American History, 84*(1), 40–66.

DeGruy-Leary, J. A. (2005). Post traumatic slave syndrome: America's legacy of enduring injury and healing. Uptone Press.

Du Bois, W. E. B. (1903). *The souls of Black folk: Essays and sketches.* A. G. McClurg.

Etis, D., & Richardson, D. (Eds.). (2015). The atlas of *the Transatlantic Slave Trade.* Yale University Press.

Gates, H. L., & Burton, J. (2008). *Call and response: Key debates in African American studies.* Norton.

Gouldner, A. (1978). The new class project, II. *Theory and Society, 6*(3), 343–389.

Helm, J. (2018, August 28). What's missing in American education. *The Washington Post.* https://www.washingtonpost.com/education/2019/08/28/historians-slavery-myths/

Homan, M. (2017). *Promoting community change.* Pearson.

Johnson, B. R. (1988). *Ella's Song.* https://www.bernicejohnsonreagon.com/2014/12/03/ellas-song/

McKenna, L. (2021, February 1) Names and identity: Nomenclature as tool of slavery and invasion. *The Irish Times.* https://www.irishtimes.com/culture/books/names-and-identity-nomenclature-as-tool-of-slavery-and-invasion-1.4474187

Morrison, F. (2016). *Social workers' communication with children and young people in practice.* The Institute for Research and Innovation in Social Sciences. https://www.iriss.org.uk/authors/dr-fiona-morrison

Ntloedibe, F. (2019). Silencing evidence: Reflections on the scholarship on African involvement in the European slave trade. *African Historical Review, 51*(2), 1–16. https://doi.org/10.1080/17532523.2019.1675297

Rawick, G. P. (1972). *From sundown to sunup: The making of Black community.* Greenwood.

Rogers, L. (2006). *Call and response: The wisdom of Rumi.* iUniverse.

Ryan, C. (2010). Engaging families to support lesbian, gay, bisexual and transgender (LGBT) youth: The Family Acceptance Project. *The Prevention Researcher, 17*(4), 11–13.

Salisbury University. (2020). *1619–2019: 400 years of resistance.* https://libraryguides.salisbury.edu/400years

Schiele, J. H. (1996). Afrocentricity: An emerging paradigm in social work practice. *Social Work, 41*(3), 284–294.

Stack, C. (1982). *All our kin.* The Free Press.

Withers, Bill. (1971). Grandma's hands. *On Just as I Am.* Booker T. Jones. https://g.co/kgs/i3wZNe

Yancy, L. (2016). *Black bodies, White gazes: The continuing significance of race in America.* Rowman & Littlefield Publishers.

Young, V. A. (2009). "Nah, we straight": An argument against code switching. *JAC, 29*(1/2), 49–76.

CHAPTER 5

Remove the Stumbling Blocks—I Want to Live and Thrive

Wisdom From the Enslaved Person Narratives for the Dominant Out-Group Domain

Introduction

Through this research it became apparent that the enslaved person narratives spoke to the inevitably constructed existence of a fourth domain exerting influence on the lives of the enslaved, emanating from the enslaver and White society at large. It is a socially constructed domain based on the reality of deeply enforced segregation economically, socially, and interpersonally (except, of course, through the coerced sexual "relationship" of rape.) Equally important and perhaps ironic is the perceived value (or not) of the relationship between enslaved and enslaver. This chapter addresses the unsettling way it was culturally congruent for the enslaved to have meaningful connections, in limited yet real ways, on the plantation with other human beings for survival—even to their oppressor.

The domain of the enslaver seems to relate to the perception and experience of interpersonal relations with them that resulted in either some favorable or profoundly unfavorable outcomes. Enslavers oppressed and controlled at will and largely dictated the fate of their inventory of enslaved people. Given the constructed nature of the enslaved–enslaver relationship, the interpersonal transactions were largely nonreciprocal and based on domination and enforced obedience. This makes sense considering the denial of personhood by White enslavers toward the enslaved Black people under their yoke.

Extending the concept of community as a way of relating to others validates the enormous psychic, social, and physical energy required to successfully engage in interpersonal relations with a community of others with absolute power over your life, particularly when the other community actively engages in activities of oppression or domination aimed at you and members of your group. Nevertheless, the formerly enslaved respondents reported four distinct protective factors in this domain that represent White out-group connections for goods and services, benevolence, protection, and opportunity for the upward mobility of formerly enslaved human beings.

Protective Factors

Goods and Services Defined as Giving Concrete Aid to Enslaved People

Many formerly enslaved respondents in the sample report that their enslaver would provide a wide range of goods and services to enslaved people related to basic needs (e.g., clothing, foodstuff, shelter, medical care). James Bolton from Georgia expressed the kinds of material aid he received from his enslaver, stating, "Now I gwine tell you the troof. Now that it's all over I don't find life so good in my old age, as it was in slavery time when I was chillum down on Marster's plantation. Then I did't have to worry 'bout whar my clothes and my somepin' to eat was comin' from or whar I was gwine to sleep. Marster tuk keer of all that."[1] Such comments need to be interpreted carefully because they were made at the height of the Depression when extreme poverty was greater for southern Black Americans than any other social group. Such statements speak to the largely unchanged living conditions of Black sharecroppers in the 1930s since the time of slavery.

Some enslaved people received even better treatment. For example, Jerry Boykins from Texas said, "I been well taken care of durin' my life. When I was young I lived right in the big house with my marster. I was houseboy."[2] In rarer cases, some enslaved people received moral support and the kind of human validation that was often missing from almost all enslaved–enslaver relationships. Anna Miller from Texas remembered her enslaver complimenting her on her worth, enough to authorize medical care: "One mornin' he (marster) comes and looks at me and say, 'dis nigger am too val'able to die. We'd better doctor her."[3]

Laura Ramsey Parker from Tennessee reported receiving land from the enslaver when emancipation had come, stating, "MR wuz mah marster en he wuz sho good ter his slaves. He treated dem as human bein's. W'en he turned his slaves 'loose he gib dem no money, but gib dem lands, clothin en food til dey could brang in dere fust crop."[4]

Many formerly enslaved people in the sample reflected on their young lives under slavery and remembered how food was available and that it was given to them in rations. Many respondents reported having had small patches of gardens for growing vegetables, and many received livestock to prepare for their families. This did not mean that such behavior was solely altruistic. Much like their care for their oxen, the enslaver needed to make certain that his workers were fed well enough to do their jobs. Irene Robertson from Arkansas says, "Had plenty to eat; meat, corncake and molasses, peas and garden stuff."[5]

Enslaved Person Narrative Excerpt

Anna Miller, 85 years old, was sold into slavery with her mother to Mark Loyed, a farmer in Missouri who then sold her to another enslaver in Palo Pinto, Texas. She was 8 years old when making the trek to Texas and took sick with the fever: "I'se so bad, de marster thinks I'se goin' to die. One mornin' he (Marster) comes and looks at me and say, 'dis nigger am too val'able to die. We'd better doctor her."

As these narratives make clear, there were occasional acts of kindness and support that in part altered relationships between the enslaved and their enslavers. We offer our own examples of this kind of experience—not to diminish the ongoing systemic racism that we too have experienced as African Americans, but to underscore that there are White people who also choose to create a story distinct from the dominant narrative of White supremacy. These small stories shine a light on the possibility for change in the lives of young people without denying the need for broader systemic change.

Barbara's Personal Experience

When I was 14 years old, I was selected to participate in the CETA program (Comprehensive and Employment Training Act) and had the opportunity to work at a comptroller's office. The office was fully staffed by White professionals. I did the filing and general office work. It was the first time I had the experience of being in that sort of work environment. One or two of the White women there took an interest in me and would ask me about school and give me guidance around the job. I was also treated to lunch a few times by these women over the course of the summer. Both could see that I was smart and had an aptitude for the general office work and that I was comfortable in the work environment. I was able to see, perhaps reluctantly but nevertheless honestly, that I could be in relationship with some White people without experiencing the degradation my mother had feared. Like the enslaved men and women in this study, I made the necessary discernment of each White person with whom I interacted.

I also remember feeling so proud that I earned a paycheck. That money came in handy for my single mom who was doing her level best to keep us in our own home.

Deborah's Personal Experience

When I attended elementary school in New York City none of the teachers looked like me, not even after they emerged fully tanned at the start of the school year, having spent whole summers on the beaches of Long Island and places south. And yet in sixth grade there appeared a young man recently arrived from Ireland. I appreciated his wonderful Irish brogue and his sense that we could all learn. It was a sense I believed in because he saw my work as comparable to that of my White peers and complimented my written work and math skills. In me he saw the kind of potential my parents always told me I had, a potential that would honestly stand up strong alongside that of any other student. Before Mr. Milner, I had never been told in a classroom that I had ability before, let alone college potential.

He encouraged me to be more productive in my work to show what I could do—me, the Black girl with two pigtails who shied away from saying much more than a few words even when coaxed. I cannot say if I remember doing anything differently, but apparently I did because the teacher with the wonderful Irish brogue spoke with my parents on a number of occasions and even stayed in touch with them throughout my high school career. This I remember with great vividness because Mr. Milner worked as an emissary on my behalf and got me into an Ivy League school when there was still a single-digit quota placed on entering Black students. Back at the age of 11, I may not have known what I wanted to do or even what I wanted to study, but because of this man, I knew that I could pursue whatever I could dream.

Benevolence Defined as the Enslaver Displaying Kindness, Charity, Empathy, and Goodwill to Enslaved People

For enslaved people, given the diminished options they had to make meaning in their world, it was better to have an enslaver who was sometimes kind than one who was not at all kind. Of course there were far more reports of very mean and vicious enslavers and their wives on plantations. But there also were some enslaved people who were able to connect with a more benevolent side of their enslavers. Eliza Ison from Kentucky said, "BW and AB were our masters. Both were good and kind to us. I never saw a slave whipped, for my boss did not believe in that kind of punishment."[6]

Eliza Williamson from Georgia shared a similar sentiment about her enslaver; she said, "He was as gentle with his slaves as a father would have been, was never known to abuse one of them."[7]

Some of the respondents discussed enslavers who helped to keep families together, before and after the war. For Mary Jane Wilson in Virginia, "Her master purchased her father from a neighboring plantation so that mother and father and daughter could live together."[8] This formerly enslaved woman went on to become one of the first Black teachers in Virginia.

After the war her enslaver's wife reunited Dianah Watson of Texas with her mother at a neighboring plantation: "That old miss carries me to G on to my mammy. She tells her to take good care of me and we lived there for three years before moving away."[9] Willis Williams from Florida remembers that his enslaver "wanted his family and servants well cared for and spared no expense in making life happy."[10]

Many formerly enslaved respondents reported overwhelming sadness at the passing of the enslaver and remembered funerals and grieving. James Bolton from

Georgia says, "I ain't never forget when Mistress died, she had been so good to every nigger on our plantation—the niggers on our plantation all walked to church to hear her funeral sermon and then walked to the graveyard to the buryin'."[11]

We need to underscore that this was not a preeminent finding from the sample of 50 men and 50 women. It was, nevertheless, significant enough in number to rise to the level of a valuable, albeit surprising, finding. Other authors have made clear not to lose sight of the larger horror at play under slavery. In fact there were enslavers who didn't resort to terror, but however benevolent their behavior, the brutality of enslavement is not overshadowed (King, 1995; Spivey, 2019). Yetman (1970) and Onion (2015) point out that at the time they were being interviewed many of the formerly enslaved people may have been reluctant to characterize the enslaver in terms of brutality rather than in Christian terms out of fear that the WPA agents might hold their words against them as they applied for benefits from the federal government. Many respondents had applied for and were awaiting news about the old age pension. This may account for the rose-colored remembrances of some of the respondents. At the same time, the consistent appearance of this trend among the randomized sample of WPA respondents suggests the need to acknowledge that in the midst of the horrific brutality of slavery there were some enslavers and enslaved people who forged enough of a relationship as to be remembered with some positive regard. Such a finding does not negate the brutality of the institution nor the trauma it unleashed for generations to come (Hannah-Jones et al., 2021). It does show that within all social groups, White and Black as well as all others, there is variability in the human spirit and the willingness to transcend at least some of the chattels and chains that constrained them all from their full humanity.

Enslaved Person Narrative Excerpt

Mary Jane Wilson, age unknown, reflected about her enslaver, who helped to keep her family together before and after the war. She was an only child and was sold with her mother to the Virginia enslaver. Her mother begged him to keep the family together and convinced him to also purchase her husband from a neighboring plantation so that mother and father and daughter could live together. Miss Wilson believed that kind act was the reason she went on to become one of the first Black teachers in Virginia. It is an act for which she, all those many years later, recalled with gratefulness.

Barbara's Personal Experience

When I was in college, that first summer semester, I was not in a good relationship with my mother. She and I had an implicit agreement that once I turned 18 I was on my own; she had done her job of raising me. My first two semesters of college were not my best years. I was poor. I had failed the first class of my academic life. I was feeling pretty low, and at semester's end I was going to be homeless. Fortunately, a White school administrator heard of my plight and carved out a solution for me that entailed some work in exchange for lodging. Such caring by a far more powerful, albeit distant, college administrator stabilized me in ways that allowed me to later flourish in college—something that otherwise would not have been possible.

Later, when I was employed as a manager for a citizen lobby organization right after college, I was offered a position in central New Jersey as a manager in a field canvassing office. I was happy to be heading home to New Jersey. When I arrived in central Jersey for my new job, I needed to find housing right away. I picked up the classified ads, made calls, and inquired about renting studios and one-bedroom apartments near my office. I set up appointments over the phone, but when I went to see the units and meet the landlords, the apartments were no longer available. "But over the phone, 30 minutes ago, you said it was vacant, and now ... its rented!" Racism had reared its head. It went on like this for months. Here's the new director, sleeping on a sofa in her office, showering at a staff member's home, and not able to find a place to live! Eventually, I did find a place, above a pizzeria. I was desperate, and the apartment wasn't ideal, but I grabbed it. The landlord was a very kind Italian man who engaged me in real talk about my housing experience. I told him the truth. He had empathy for my situation, which allowed me to relax and feel secure where I was now living.[i]

Protection Defined as the Enslaver's Role in Protecting the Enslaved Person from Harm

Anthony Taylor from Arkansas summed up in a simple statement one of the truths of antebellum life: "Wasn't no law then. He (master) was the law."[12] The protection, however ignoble, extended to adults and children alike, according to James Bolton from Georgia: "In slavery time chilluns weren't 'llowed to do no wuk kazen the marsters wanted they niggers to grow up big and strong and didn' want 'em stunted none."[13]

---

i After I was housed, I immediately joined an organization to do test cases for violations of housing statutes. A coworker and I were testers. She was White, and I am Black. We made calls to landlords suspected of violating the rights of Black people seeking housing. We presented profiles to the landlord, education, employment, earnings, and so on that were identical; the only difference would be she was White and I was Black. This methodology was successful in holding racist landlords accountable who violated housing discrimination laws. Housing insecurity has plagued me all my adult life and is stressful. Choosing to be a social worker and to work in the trenches oftentimes means that my salary does not keep pace with inflation. And even as I continue to make more and more investments into my professional and academic credentials, my salary doesn't increase in proportionate ways. Housing for working-class people is often substandard, and laws tend to favor the owner rather than the leased tenants. Even into my 60s I can be forced to leave my home after a 2-year lease is over.

Some enslaved respondents reported being spared the brutality of the nightriders. Witness the statement of George Henderson from Kentucky: "I have heard the Klu Klux Klan ride down the road wearing masks. None ever bothered me or any of Marse Cleveland's slaves."[14] Anthony Taylor from Arkansas says the same: "Where we was, the Ku Kluz never did bother anybody, all there was, every time we went out we had to have a pass from marse and we was ok."[15]

Another report spoke of actual kindness. An enslaved child, Lucindia Washington from Alabama, had a harrowing encounter with a snake in a meadow at a neighboring plantation, and after the ordeal she "decided to rest at the foot of a tree for only a moment, but fell asleep. A couple of hours later it was twilight and the overseer walking through the woods and came upon the Negro girl. He lifted the small black form into his arms and carried her safely to the house."[16]

In this realm of physical security, most enslaved people understood the ways of the South and the ways of bondage: if master wanted you dead, it would be made so. Connecting to the enslaver along with the other layers of protective factors, beginning with the internal connections in Chapter 2 through family and enslaved community, could literally mean the difference between life and death—of which only some small part was in your control. Understanding this truth and the enslaved people's capacity to find some agency and control under dire circumstances is a lesson passed on, unfortunately yet necessarily, when Black parents have "the talk" with their children about how to survive the mean streets of every American community.

Enslaved Person Narrative Excerpt

Mr. George Henderson, 77 years old, lived on "Marse" Cleveland's plantation. He reported being spared the brutality of the patty rollers and the nightriders in the year following the end of the Civil War: "I have heard the Klu Klux Klan ride down the road wearing masks. None ever bothered me or any of the Marse Cleveland's slaves."

Barbara's Personal Experience

I put a Black Lives Matter sign in my window and in the window of my car during the height of the George Floyd protests in 2020. Several White neighbors questioned me about it both directly and indirectly through a community Facebook page. My wife and I organized single-car caravans in support of the protests so that we could be safe from COVID-19 and be part of the movement. We wrote letters to the editor in our local paper, and the pushback from citizens was oftentimes unkind and scary. In fact, during one caravan ride, a car with two White men in it pulled up next to us and started giving us the finger and calling my wife, who is White, a nigger lover and me a nigger.

Just the sign, Black Lives Matter, invoked that White rage. The local police department regularly meets with our community, and at the next community meeting following this encounter, I posed a question to the chief of police related to the fear I was feeling from simply exercising my right to free speech, protest, and grievance as an American citizen. We were all seated in the parking lot of our community complex when I stood to ask my question. The chief of police said that it was their duty to uphold the law, that no one had the right to infringe on my rights, and that if any one threatened me in any way to call them and they would handle the matter. Then he made a generalized statement to the entire community about diversity and respect of one another. Afterward several White neighbors came up to me and thanked me for the question and for my activism and courage to stand up. While hardly addressing the underlying structural issues that lead to such extreme acts of intimidation directed at Black and Brown people (and, occasionally, their White allies and partners), such kindness and support—not unlike the occasional actions mentioned by the formerly enslaved people—can help smooth an otherwise barren and crater-filled path that so many people of color have always walked in America.

Opportunity Defined as a Chance for Advancement, Betterment, or Progress

Sometimes the enslaver allowed the enslaved to learn trades and special skills; Irene Robertson from Arkansas tells of her opportunity: 'They trained black women to be midwives."[17]

A common experience for the highly skilled enslaved person was the practice of loaning out the skilled worker to other White people in the community. Through this practice some enslaved people occasionally benefited economically, as was the case with Henry Wright from Georgia:

> "Mr. House wanted his slaves to learn a trade such as masonry or carpentry, etc., not because it would benefit the slave, but because it would make the slave sell for more in case he had get shet [rid] of him. The slaves who were allowed to work with these White mechanics from who they eventually learned the trade, were eager because they would be permitted to hire themselves out. The money they earned could be used to help buy their freedom, that is, what money remained after the master had taken his share."[18]

Likewise, Maria Sutton Clements from Arkansas stated, "The missus showed the nigger women how to sow. All the women on the place could card and spin."[19]

The following excerpt is about an experience immediately after the war ended. America Morgan from Indiana stated, "When I was 13 years old, I did not know A from B, then glory to god, a white man, from the north, came to town and opened a school for negro children, that was my firs chance to learn."[20] From that point she integrated education in to her life and the lives of her children.

Bert Mayfield from Kentucky says, "My old Mistus taught me how to read from an old national spelling book."[21] He was so pleased to get the learning because he knew that he now had advantage over so many others who did not know their letters. "My mistis teached me how to reed,"[22] says Isaac Stier from Mississippi. He expressed profound gratitude for her tutelage because he knew that helped him to be successful in his life after emancipation. When enslaved people connected to opportunity they made the best of the chance, and for some the benefits compounded over their life span. They realized that these small shards of opportunity could alter their lives' trajectory. This speaks to the inherent agency of these human beings, no matter the constraints of bondage.

Enslaved Person Narrative Excerpt

Isaac Stier, 99 years old and from Mississippi, said, "My mistis, Miss Sarah Stowers, teached me how to read and she taught me how to be mannerly too." He expressed profound gratitude for her tutelage because he knew that helped him to be successful in his life after emancipation. Mr. Stier was very loyal to the family that enslaved him. He was a coachman and a play companion to the children in the big house. After fighting side by side with his enslaver in the war, he was captured by the Yankees in Vicksburg and fought with them until 1866. When the war ended he returned to the land of his enslaver and began to sharecrop the land. He married and made a living farming chickens and the land all the rest of his life. At the time of the interview with the WPA agent, Mr. Stier was under the care of a doctor who was the grandson of his enslaver.

Barbara's Personal Experience

When I graduated from high school, I had a number of scholarships based on academics and athletics. Had I not had those scholarships to help with room, board, tuition, and books, I would not have been able to see my way to college. I did qualify for financial aid based on my mom's earnings. Truthfully, like many students, that financial aid was the money I needed to live on while in college. Had I not made it to college, my life would have taken a different trajectory. I am not advocating that everyone should go to college, but for me that was a dream I wanted to fulfill. I know it was an expectation of my mother's. She sacrificed plenty for me to get there. I knew it would make her and my grandmother very proud.

College opened the door for me to create more opportunity for myself. I started out as a pre-med student but changed course when it became clear to me that the pathway would be riddled with unnecessary and unwelcomed hurdles that were not erected for my White counterparts on the pre-med tract. For example, my essays were more closely scrutinized for grammar and punctuation. I also experienced conflicts between work study hours and hours for labs for my freshman seminar in biology. I had to work because I had no money, and yet neither the professor nor the supervisor was flexible enough to accommodate my needs. This filled me with anger and caused me to rethink the profession I wanted to enter. I was lost for a little while, then landed on the notion that I could become a social worker. After meeting with the chair of the social work department at my college, I knew

I had found a place for my anger and my sense of righteous indignation about the injustices in the world. I changed my major to social worker and never looked back.

Deborah's Personal Experience

I had worked in a public child welfare agency for some time, finding the work meaningful but my immediate supervisors less than capable of keeping the interests of at-risk youth forward —one anxious about always pleasing her own boss, even when data showed children being underserved; the other more concerned about her appearance and "presenting well" than the work itself. The final boss who caused me to resign made the others look benign. To maintain program continuity, I was given the responsibility to locate additional funds to assist young people in our care with the resources needed to attend wraparound support services and to generate additional program materials for the Youth Savings and Asset Building program. I managed to procure funding from our financial partners for just that purpose.

My boss, who previously had made a citywide reputation as an advocate for children, refused to accept the funds because there was too much paperwork involved—and my name rather than hers appeared on the grant. No amount of pleading helped, nor did the fact that these young people would lose out on a chance to improve their executive skills. Fed up, I put in my resignation the next day.

Luckily, the head of a nonprofit agency, Laura Trayner, who was overseeing a senior retraining program, and was a champion for aging in place, learned of my efforts in collaboration with public and private partners, and on the day I resigned, she reached out to offer me a job. I was at work at ReServe the next week, happily developing new training programs, arranging scheduling, and recruiting trainers. About 2 months later, Ms. Trayner had to be hospitalized for a serious operation and treatment. Having seen the quality of my work as well as engagement in the work firsthand, this White woman asked that I serve as acting director in her stead. As her illness and ensuing condition became more prolonged, she again asked that I stay on, making certain I was given credit for my work to her funders and her board.

She had known I loved to work with young people and that my stay would not be permanent, but her faith in me led me to stay on until she was finally able to return. By then, others at the public child welfare agency had noticed my work, and an associate commissioner, (now the late) Iris Kaplan (a Jewish woman from Brooklyn), reached out and asked me to join her team in what proved to be another job with real opportunity working on youth leadership, education, and other tasks of inherent responsibility. A circle of mutual respect, support, and hard work, all in service to our young people, had been created at long last!

The Sankofa Guidance for Practitioners and Educators: Working with White Allies and Officials

The enslaver dominant community protective factors that promote resilience were connections to goods and services, benevolence, protection, and opportunity. Pause for a moment. To young Black and Brown people, what is the "master community" in the 21st century? It would be naïve to suggest that there are not complexities related to a modern-day interpretation of this domain; just as it would be untrue to say that *all* enslavers were White. It would be equally untrue to suggest that only White people are members of the out-group in contemporary society. What matters most is how the African American youth defines the out- group and who they assign to that category. That has implications about the connection and what types of protections will be needed from the connection.

The analysis of the use of this domain's finding will be put forward based on the understanding that the enslaver domain today is represented by White Americans, most of whom enjoy privilege in American society. It is the domain of the dominant culture, the culture of European ethnocentrism represented by White Americans, own or control most of the goods and services. White Americans run most of the companies and thus employ the workers and provide the jobs. White Americans are in the position to provide not just individualized forms of charity and second chances but redistributions of wealth and genuine reparations. While of course young Black and Brown people are not waiting for help, let's be clear: White Americans can provide real protection from the dangers associated with life in high-risk environments—not by their presence but by their recognition that true inequities must and will be addressed. People denied opportunity and access to wealth creation still need their 40 acres and a low-cost mortgage, not a mule!

At the same time, there also are important choices for both the youth and members of the out-group that can either constrain or facilitate their own resilience. For African American youth, there is a need to master competence in the area of judgment as it relates to discerning which White person or persons from the out-group can provide the goods, charity, opportunity, and protection they also offer younger White people. This cognitive process will require a shifting of a paradigm from "all members of the out-group are my enemy" to the realization that holding conspiratorial thoughts can constrain resilience. Academic skills are not "White." Learning such skills as critical thinking, logic, and writing harken back not just to London and Paris but to Accra and Alexandria. Black and Brown adults who support young people must make that clear.

Based on the findings from this research, a new way of thinking is to realize the urgency of pressing ahead and taking the risk to reach out across racial lines, across geographic barriers, to seek help and support. Learning to fine tune judgment about people happens over the course of maturation. At-risk youth may need supports in strengthening the internal barometer about which advocacy they accept as assistance. One is not turning away from one's own community to state that young people will need to learn to trust some in the out-group in order to move forward.

For members of the dominant out-group, there are choices when encountering African American youth, from the initial appraisal through the duration of the social and professional interaction. The choice has to do with "will I or won't I" be part of this young person's resilience narrative? Is there some opportunity I can provide? Are there some goods or services I can bring to bear that could make a difference? Is there some protection they need from me? Is there some kind of charity that can remedy some specific need? In this way, members of the out-group can choose to distribute their personal advantage to help bridge the cavernous gaps of human interactions created by historical disparity. In this way, as they choose to redistribute goods, services, opportunity, and charity, each according to their ability, one child at a time can be further moved along the continuum of resilience, from surviving to thriving.

Advocacy at the Micro, Meso, and Macro Levels

At the same time, there are innumerable specific actions that professionals can take at every level of advocacy and that can make a profound difference in the lives of young people. The ones we offer are those that over our professional careers we ourselves have utilized—not all at once, but over many years. We offer this simple approach to help you decide how to undertake them (as well as your own!) guided by three simple principles in your advocacy work:

- **Add in; don't add on:** See advocacy as integral to your work, not an add-on that one does on occasion.
- **Consistency, not constancy:** Your work will not allow full-time, constant advocacy; at the same time, consistent "chipping away" at each of these levels is a way for you and the young people you work with to target the organizational (meso) and systemic (macro) levels that are also part of the history and context that impact the lives of your clients.
- **You don't have to do a lot; you must do a little:** Trust, openness to problem solving, and strong relationships are not built in one fell swoop but through a willingness to do the small things with consistency in your work over a lifetime of relationships with people with whom you work.

Work to Be Undertaken at the Micro and Meso Levels (Reforms and Activities at the Practice and Program Level)

Examples of Direct individual advocacy:

- access to quality and affordable foods
- access to affordable housing
- quality clothing
- access to preschool
- support to complete all of K–12
- support/access to higher education

- access to after-school activities
- recreational spaces
- advocacy for affordable health care
- meaningful social spaces for students and client
- antiharassment and antibullying school programs/policies
- summer camps
- exchange programs
- tuition remission programs (location and advocacy)

Advocacy at the meso level:

- mental health clinics
- drug treatment centers, utility and energy support, and childcare subsidies
- arts and music education
- family planning assistance
- exposure for young people to civics and the importance of citizenship
- shelters and supportive housing for abuse victims
- diversity-sensitivity training
- antiracism training
- alliance for interrupting systemic and personal acts of racism
- hiring formerly incarcerated persons
- banning the box that convicted felons must check on all job applications

Advocating for Policies, Programs, and Practices That Protect and Ensure the Safety of Black Youth

Examples of legislative and campaign advocacy:

- community policing
- civilian review boards
- clean water/clean air
- investment in mass transit and transportation
- guaranteed enfranchisement
- fair share taxation
- ending the school-to-prison pipeline
- reforming outdated child welfare laws
- gun control
- gun buyback programs
- diversion programs
- gang interdiction programs
- ending of racial profiling
- tenants' rights
- ending of disparities in drug laws
- needle exchange program creation
- human trafficking prevention

- expansion of HIV prevention programs
- vaccinations and preventative medications
- LGBTQI+ protections
- consumer protection laws
- reparations support
- support for better funding for public education
- historically Black colleges and universities support
- investment in public libraries
- support for Black-owned business
- support for Black artists
- support for civil rights organizations
- expansion of voter rights

Concluding Comment

We are well aware of the complexity and potentially combustible material contained in this chapter. Make no mistake: it is not added as a positive coda to an otherwise horrific experience, thus proverbially or otherwise "whitewashing" the American stain of slavery away. That said, to ignore these findings because they do not conform to the unidimensional narrative of only unrelieved suffering would do a disservice to the inherent agency of the enslaved people attempting to carve out a life of some safety and purpose in the midst of horror. As Edward P. Jones (2004) makes clear in his brilliant novel *The Known World*, people whose lives never knew "lived experience" beyond a 10-mile circumference of plantation, dirt roads, and (perhaps) a general store nevertheless sought out ways to live based on whatever they *could* know. Lacking the future telegraph, telephone, radio, television, the internet, and even the opportunity to read the written word, they still constructed a way to live.

That some chose to discern differences in types of enslavers or took appreciation from the modest gifts occasionally bestowed were not acts of deference but measures of meaning to make their lives livable. To locate these snippets of appreciation and thanks within the context of horrific exploitation is to admire the dignity and grace inherent in their own stories. Every Black American has such a story as well—perhaps not quite so horrific as for those once enslaved, but a mixture of pride and sorrow, of opportunity denied and resilience realized in spite of the adversity. In affirming the beauty and complexity of our forebearers, we affirm ourselves and the young ones among us seeking guidance. When we pronounce that we stand on the shoulders of our ancestors, we share the courage, brilliance, and strength of their stories with those who today seek to create a new and better future for themselves.

Endnotes

Excerpts from the Federal Writers' Project Slave Narrative (FWPSN) Collection

1. FWPSN, Georgia, Part 1, p. 104
2. FWPSN, Texas, Part 1, p. 121
3. FWPSN, Texas, Part 3, p. 82
4. FWPSN, Tennessee, p. 62
5. FWPSN, Arkansas, Part 2, p. 15
6. FWPSN, Kentucky, p. 2
7. FWPSN, Georgia, Part 4, p. 148
8. FWPSN, Virginia, p. 55
9. FWPSN, Texas, Part 4, p. 146
10. FWPSN, Florida, p. 350
11. FWPSN, Georgia, Part 1, p. 92
12. FWPSN, Arkansas, Part 6, p. 260
13. FWPSN, Georgia, Part 1, p. 95
14. FWPSN, Kentucky, p. 7
15. FWPSN, Arkansas, Part 6, p. 260
16. FWPSN, Alabama, p. 409
17. FWPSN, Arkansas, Part 7, p. 232
18. FWPSN, Georgia, Part 4, p. 196
19. FWPSN, Arkansas, Part 2, p. 17
20. FWPSN, Indiana, p. 142
21. FWPSN, Kentucky, p. 15
22. FWPSN, Mississippi, p. 145

References

Hannah-Jones, N., Roper, C., Silverman, I., & Silverberg, H. (2021). *The 1619 project: A new origin story*. Random House One World Imprint Press.

Jones, E. P. (2004). *The known world*. Amistad.

King, W. (1995). *Stolen childhood: Slave youth in 19th-century America*. Indiana University Press.

Onion, R. (2015). Is the greatest collection of slave narratives tainted? *Slate*. http://www.slate.com/articles/news_and_politics/history/2016/07/can_wpa_slave_narratives_be_trusted_or_are_they_tainted_by_depression_era.html

Spivey, W. (2019). The fallacy of "good" slave owners. *Dialogue and Discourse https://medium.com/discourse/the-fallacy-of-good-slave-owners-7dd2ea2dad2f.*

Yetman, N. R. (1970). *Voices from slavery*. Dover Publications, Inc.

■ CHAPTER 6

The Enduring Pain of Enslavement

"Joy Cometh in the Morning"

Although slavery has long been a part of human history, American chattel slavery represents a case of human trauma incomparable in scope, duration and consequence to any other incidence of human enslavement.

—Joy DeGruy

You must resist the common urge toward the comforting narrative of divine law, toward fairy tales that imply some irrepressible justice. The enslaved were not bricks in your road, and their lives were not chapters in your redemptive history. They were people turned to fuel for the American machine. Enslavement was not destined to end, and it is wrong to claim our present circumstance—no matter how improved—as the redemption for the lives of people who never asked for the posthumous, untouchable glory of dying for their children. Our triumphs can never compensate for this.

—Ta-Nehisi Coates

I'm so tired of waiting, aren't you, for the world to become good and beautiful and kind?

—Langston Hughes

Real radicalism implores us to tell the whole ugly truth, even when it is inconvenient. To own the hurt and the pain. To own our shit, too. To think about it systemically and collectively, but never to diminish the import of the trauma.

—Brittney Cooper

Children can't see their budding lives through the long lens of wisdom—the wisdom that benefits from years passed, hurdles overcome, strength summoned, resilience realized, selves discovered and accepted, hearts broken but mended and love experienced in the fullest, truest majesty that the word deserves. For them, the weight of ridicule and ostracism can feel crushing and without the possibility of reprieve. And, in that dark and lonely place, desperate and confused, they can make horrible decisions that can't be undone.

—Charles M. Blow

Failure is an important part of your growth and developing resilience. Don't be afraid to fail.

—Michelle Obama

There is always light. If only we're brave enough to see it. If only we're brave enough to be it.

—Amanda Gorman

Hope is a song in a weary throat.

—Pauli Murray

Introduction

The substance of this book is built on the hard-won insight and wisdom of enslaved human beings whose voices were all too often ignored for all that they have given us. Using their words as our guide, we end this book by beginning with our own words, which, while not as hard-won as those our enslaved ancestors, nevertheless come from the same Black American story of pain and possibility. The first part of the conversation is what we hope is a courageous one with our Black community. The second is an equally courageous one with our White allies.

To reiterate, the simple intention of the book is to save the lives of Black and Brown youth by connecting them to the wisdom of their ancestors. We are human. That whole "say our names" theme has been developed through this book as well. *We are human.*

Before we begin our discussion, it is also important to restate the specific resilience protective factors that form the main sections of Chapters 2–5. These factors are derived from their once-enslaved ancestors for the benefit of Black and Brown youth, their families, the communities in which they live, and for White folks and other allies.

Protective factors:

- internal connections in the individual domain to power, competence, spirituality, and passion
- familial connections in the family domain to care, counsel, modeling, and rituals
- in-group connections in the Black community domain to support, opportunity, pride, and norms
- out-group connections in the White community domain to goods and services, benevolence, protection, and opportunity

Lessons From Our Ancestors Lived and Learned; Hard Truths to Hold—A Courageous Conversation With Our Black Community

Barbara: Because the title of this chapter is "Joy Cometh in the Morning," I thought we should probably reflect again on the pain and trauma that we're remedying with this book and highlight again the disparities and negative outcomes for Black youth.

If we have no intervention, no intercession, no action at all, what will the trajectory of Black youth be? These protective factors are based on the wisdom of the ancestors and are cultural nuggets of life-saving information that we're going to put in the hands of educators and social workers. Let's say again: This is what it's going to look like.

This is what it is, and now our vision is for Black youth to find their resilience and their joy by applying these principles, applying these protective factors. I think that's one of the core themes we're trying present: It's not just the pain that we experienced in enslavement and the trauma and all of that, but that resilience, that strength that comes through as well. We do have to tether this generation of youth to that strength as we push on. It's like Harriet Tubman said, "You keep on keeping on no matter what. You just keep on keeping on."

Just keep on keeping on because everything is systematically designed to keep Black folk down, to keep us oppressed, to keep us second class, to deny, deny, deny our experience as Black people, and it has always been so. We have all these amazing examples of how we press through, how we rise anyway—the simple "and yet we rise," like Maya Angelou said, right? And still we rise. You know what I mean? That message has to come through as well, and that is what we're saying.

Deborah: And while it is hard to stand up against the person who is signing your check, because without it you cannot feed and care for your family, still, use your voice and intentionally walk alongside each other, stand up for each other, and intentionally share the way to success.

Barbara: And some of that rising up, which is cultural reality, is something that's been missing when we get back to that domain of the Black community; there's the hard truth where some of us have abandoned one another. There is just too much of the "crab in the barrel" syndrome, right? Everybody's trying to get out and to the top and not helping to pull other people up and out too. Too many of us are not reaching back and bringing people with us. It's hard to say, but all too often we've adopted the European mindset of individual ruggedness, which is our death. So we've got to get back to the roots of understanding our connection to one another. My success is your success! It's the Ubuntu principle: we rise together. We're responsible for one another's success. My pride and joy comes from not just my success, but yours as well, and it's my responsibility to help you get there. Too many of us have abandoned that.

We can't buy in to the same mindset of systems that have been run by the dominant culture, like in education and every other sort of medium, where it's all competition, competition, Darwinism, that mindset of survival of the fittest. We've got to call people out on that, whatever their background. If you want to have success with Black youth, Black families, you have to abandon the competition mindset. You've got to get into the cooperative, collaborative mindset where you're building community, not building competition. If all we foster is competition across one system and the next, all we're fostering is our own death.

Deborah: With the competition of sports, albeit there is the collaborative team agenda as the driving force, still, the amount of revenue that is realized through competitive sports is not a shared collaborative—not when it comes to wealth.

Barbara: All of this also reminded me of Charles Blow of *The New York Times*, who is on a crusade talking about the truth about incest. He's telling his story and alerting the community that incest and sexual assault are not stranger rapes. It's more often your relatives. It's your friend. It's people in your home. That's where it happens. That got me to thinking about the safety of our kids in their homes. We have to be serious about protecting our children from all forms of harm. Too many Black kids are undersupervised and overparented. I think those issues are things we do to our children that are detrimental. We give them way too much responsibility, way too soon.

Deborah: Parents need to take advantage of the resources around them, and if they cannot find what they need, they should contact their local elected officials so that their children can develop an ease toward adulthood.

Barbara: We call our 9-year-old boys men. And then you wonder why they are going around trying to have sex at 10; it's because you've already knighted them as men, you don't monitor their TV viewing, and you don't talk to them. Do you know how many teenage girls I worked with over the years in my practice who did not know their anatomy, did not know about menstruation, did not know about ovaries and uteruses, and so on? And boys didn't know what a testicle was! We have to pay attention to this hard truth: I just think we fail our kids in so many ways in our families—Black, Brown, White—around protection, supervision, and education around some of these issues.

Deborah: I've seen this in schools and in child welfare. As parents we tend to assume growth and maturation in young people long before it emerges in its natural form.

Barbara: I feel compelled morally to say that safety is the responsibility of parents and the community. We have to step up and protect our children. If we stop the incest, if we stop the rape, if we stop the abuse, and instead truly protect our kids and arm them with knowledge and skills, we can then eliminate so much of the pain in their lives. If we do that, attacking the larger systemic problems will become clearer and easier.

Deborah: We need to intentionally parent, as mothers and fathers, and not intend to.

Barbara: You just said something that reminded me of my mother. It was so interesting what you just said, because it just triggered something for me. And it's about the word *joy*. And I did not experience much joy with my mom, true joy, the real feeling of "joy", until the last 6 months of her life. My entire relationship and the way that manifested was to resolve so much of the past hurts and resentments, some of which were our own making and some of which were the making of just us living our lives as Black women, as lesbian women, as poor women, as working-class women over 50 years and being beaten down by a system with each of us doing our best to survive. Just like our ancestors!

Deborah: You're saying that, and we're putting a name on it. It's like all of a sudden, you're going ... it's like the courageous conversation. Like, you have it, but it's the aha moment. We can have all the conversations in the world, but when you get that aha moment, as either Richard Pryor or Robin Williams said, there is a certain joy that comes from pain.

Barbara: Right! And some of it was about my mom being 14 at my birth and me being an unwanted child: never bonded, never securely attached, separated from her at birth for the first 9 years of my life. There were real blockages to joy and love with my mother, and those last 6 months I got it back because we resolved so much of it. And we put things in more context. And it just makes me think about our Black youth. As Joy DeGruy wrote in in her description of posttraumatic slave syndrome: one of the effects on young people from this kind of generational trauma is *that hardened look* in them. It's like you rarely see joy on the faces of our children. They're hardened, hardened by the world. They got a lot of stuff inside of them, big stuff they're reckoning with all the time. Stuff they shouldn't be reckoning with. They're defending. They're in harsh environments. They're under surveillance 24/7. All these things.

Deborah: Absolutely! If we can filter some of the realities for some children, let's do it for all children. Childhood should be protected.

Barbara: My God, I like that feeling of joy; it is beautiful. I'm 62 and I feel joy, today, deep down in in my soul. It's been a long time coming. You know what I mean; my experience is not uncommon. Would we know joy if we found it? Yes. Just like our enslaved ancestors, we should keep on keeping on until we find it. That's our mission.

We have to keep moving children toward their joy, keep moving our youth toward joy. Yeah, let's get them on the path to things like academic excellence—of course—and other success as well. But we are talking about the state of their souls. We're talking about their essence, like feeling it deep inside. That's what makes you hold your head up in the morning. That's what gets you up out of bed. That's what gives you the verve for living, which is what I have now. I never had that. And I can see that however much it was denied our enslaved ancestors, they found a way to hold their heads up, too.

Deborah: It is that universal sense of humanity, that defining quality of dignity and respect for all, that undeniable open classroom where learning is multidirectional and because of that it really, truly is possible in all schools and agencies: for all of *us*, too.

Barbara: Well, and I always say this too: With love, anything is possible. It's not that original; it's from scripture: "With Jesus, anything is possible, for God, all things are possible." I don't know if it was just conveniently substituted out, but never underestimate the value of love. That's what this book is talking about too. We've got to love Black kids. We've got to love them. We've got to love them every way we can.

Deborah: It is interesting that love is often selective depending on who holds the ruling gavel. I remember teachers complaining about students in the after-school program being unruly and messy, and these were the same children they cared for in their classrooms during the regular school day.

Barbara: Love them up, and not just tough love. We talked about that in that first domain; we need all the expression of love, unfettered, unconditional love. That's what we need more of for our kids. We need to say that in this chapter too and reinforce that. Joy and love are connected.

So much of what we've done in this book is operationalizing love, really.

It's a shame, though, we had to wait until our 60s and 70s to get that feeling inside our souls. Isn't it?

Well, it's an extraordinary waste of energy and time, isn't it? What we have to use to fend off all the cruelties of our lives, just because we're in Black skin, or live in a certain neighborhood, or go to a certain kind of school in our neighborhoods. Not for nothing else. We just waste a lot of mental energy, and it's exhausting.

Well, and that's the struggle. Eliminating racism. That's what we're all trying to do. Raising awareness about it, look what's happened, just raising awareness about racism and the pushback on it, right now. That's the struggle we're all engaged in right now, to fight that inside and outside our communities. Racism saps your joy.

Deborah: Yes, the struggle goes on—but let us please continue and spread the conversations to be courageous and inclusive: Invite everyone. It is a process with many stakeholders. Let us stay in this together and reap equity of opportunity for all youth.

Hard Truths the White Community Must Confront

Barbara: Going back to the economic roots of enslavement, it always comes back to the money. Money concentrated at the top leads to wealth, and that wealth creates investments in the structures of oppression, corporations and institutions that perpetuate the oppression of Black people. The plight of Black youth in America can only be fundamentally changed for the better if Black families have pathways to wealth. Today the average Black household has $6,000 in wealth while the average White household has $144,000. This speaks to systemic unfairness that has to change.

Deborah: The same wealth inequities exist in our school systems. How can children believe they are worth enough when their schools have no labs, old books, and leaky ceilings when 20 miles away White students study in warm, bright, and modern buildings with the best equipment and curriculum? This is not ours to correct alone.

Given what is happening in education, we know critical race theory is not being taught in elementary and high schools around the nation—it's been perverted as anti-White when all that is sought is to tell the full truth of American history and not a romanticized vision that bleaches away facts of what happened over generations. We need White allies to step up at school board meetings and support the truth of American history being taught in the classroom

Barbara: White communities must confront wealth inequity and face the truth so that real healing can begin across every community. The thing is that racism damages all our souls. And its eradication will free us all. We all have work to do!

Deborah: Amen!

Implementing the Protective Factors Through Guidance and Direction

While the systemic issues of wealth disparity and educational inequity need to be addressed, we cannot wait for these longer term structural issues to be resolved while working with the Black and Brown children in need of our support and guidance right now. We believe implementing the 16 protective factors will help transform the collective rage and despair of Black youth into peace and put our precious progeny of formally enslaved men and women on a trajectory of resilience that will generate pride and joy for themselves and for us all.

This can only happen when Black youth are seen, heard, valued, and loved as the fully entitled human beings that they, like their enslaved ancestors, always have been.

Implications for Professional Social Workers and Educators

There are many lessons about resilience contained in the narratives of enslaved people. These human beings developed awareness, knowledge, and skills that increased their chances of survival during their enslavement. In order to create change and for the lives of their progeny to improve we must begin with admitting that racism still exists in America and that it has damaging effects on its intended targets. As both our ancestors and our own stories make clear, African Americans continue to experience oppression and continue to be vulnerable to its deleterious effect. One significant casualty of racism and oppression is the loss of the ability to connect to other human beings for the support that is needed to overcome adversity. As practitioners and researchers, we can take steps to increase the resilience of African American youth who succumb far too often to the exposure to trauma and other risks in their homes and communities.

Social workers are uniquely equipped to take on this challenge at the individual, family, and community levels, as well as through research. Social work services need to be delivered in culturally responsive and sensitive ways. Cultural humility is about knowledge, values, and skills (Diller, 2007). Cultural humility does not mean that only Black people can serve Black people, that only Latinx can serve Latinx, or that only gay people can serve gay people (Taylor-Brown et al., 2001). Cultural humility is about more than the ethnic matching of practitioner to client. The orientation to intervention is more dialectical: A person can be White and also be helpful in eradicating racism; a client can be in pain and still be resilient.

A culturally humble practitioner will operate from the value of respectfulness of the other and in partnership with others across from them. We thus seek to develop culturally congruent skills to gain some mastery over obstacles that otherwise can all too often impede resilience and well-being. Cultural humility requires that the provider of services incorporates a wider lens through which to frame culturally sensitive assessment and interventions and to deliver the service in a manner that upholds the dignity of the client. The following section will highlight interventions aimed at strengthening resilience for African American youth. Utilizing lessons from their enslaved ancestors can be a powerful part of such interventions.

For Practice in Clinical and Educational Settings

At the individual level of practice, empowerment, skill building, hope, and motivation can be powerful tools for intervention. As a first step, clinicians and educators working with African American youth can affirm and validate the existence of racism as a debilitating force working against African American resilience. Young people need to know that social workers and teachers understand something about racism. They also need to be affirmed that their own story will be the definitive story about how racism operates in their lives. Instead of shying away from the enslaved past, that means sharing these stories as well—a brutal world of enslavement yet with a people strong enough to create their own meaningful way forward.

Furthermore, it is important to talk about the white elephant in the room—whether in a classroom setting or an agency office. A hallmark of culturally humble assessment is to get at "the impact of culture, historical experiences, individual and group oppression, adjustment styles, worldviews and specific cultural customs and practice, definitions and beliefs about the causation of wellness and illness and how care and services should be delivered" (NASW, 2001, para. 3).

Paradoxically, by not shying away from the pain, a social worker or teacher opens the possibility of a young person's triumph. Knowing and acknowledging the parameters of impact caused by historical and current trauma operating in their lives sets the stage of reconnecting young people to the legacy of their resilience. Classrooms can become alive to hurt and to how worthwhile it can be to overcome it. Individual sessions explore stories of similar hurts yet create openings for self-exploration and positive expression. This can be achieved by an approach that increases personal agency and power, strengthens internal locus of control, challenges negative thinking, and affirms their value as human beings. What better way to affirm these strengths than locating them among people once kept in bondage but never broken?

There also is some intellectual movement afoot regarding developing clinical constructs that would validate the etiological impact of racism and historical oppression on the formation of psychiatric and clinical syndromes and disorders. We would like to build evidence for such a construct as *post-traumatic slave syndrome* (PTSS; DeGruy, 2005) by testing for the presence of PTSS symptoms among cohorts of African American youth and delineating them in future diagnostic criteria, including the eventual DSM-VI. Such diagnostic tools should register racism and racial discrimination as legitimate symptoms of affective and neurotic conditions that affect African Americans and other people of color.

Resilience research is a relatively new area of research and presents many new opportunities for scholars. Qualitative researchers working on historical trauma, intergenerational trauma, racism, oppression, and African American well-being from a social work orientation will benefit greatly from cross-discipline collaboration with various other academic departments, from sociology to anthropology. This cross-fertilization of ideas and scholarship can help continue the emancipation process of our African American clients. Such a unified effort seems required if we are to create a world free of suffering. As long as racism and oppression thrive, all life suffers.

At the time of the interview with the Writers' Writers Project, formerly enslaved African Americans were still looking for some assistance from the larger European American society but had few illusions about their prospects. As Mary Divine from Missouri explained, "I git what de relief pretend to call help, tain't nuff for nothin' though. De claim I'll git a pension, but I never seen it yet. I'll be dead directly and I won't need it."[1] Jane Sutton from Mississippi said, "I's old an' needy, but I's trustin' de Lord an 'de good white folks to he'p me now."[2] The formerly enslaved men and women who participated in those WPA interviews did their part; they survived the brutality of slavery and lived to tell about it.

This historical study utilized a sample of the FWP enslaved person narratives and yielded findings from 100 representative men and women about protective factors and resilience. These narratives confirmed that African Americans' resilience while enslaved is reflective of a cultural axiology requiring connections to many others for survival. The internal and external connections have been further defined by 16 specific protective factors, some defined as personal coping strengths and others as familial, in-group, and out-group connections. African American youth from high-risk environments today need the largest possible repertoire of protective factors.

As with enslaved people, our work with individuals is an important yet incomplete part of their liberation. Enslaved people understood that emancipation was only the beginning. As Rachel Harris of Arkansas said, "I sho was glad they had that war and freed me, with mo'to do."[3]

The battle for social, economic, and racial justice continues in America. Far too many African American youth reside in communities that deny them a legitimate opportunity for mobility, the full range of civil rights and freedoms, and the dignity and respect required to internalize esteem and self-love, essential ingredients for health and healing. Social workers can provide the leadership required in practice, policy, advocacy, and research to rally allies and liberate resources necessary to make real the promise of African American emancipation from the vestiges of historical trauma.

Sarah Pittman from Arkansas says, "We are waiting on the promises of the God."[4] In the meantime, educators and social workers can use the history of the once unheard to inform their short- and long-term interventions with Black youth. Black youth are worthy of life, liberty and the pursuit of happiness too. Lifting up Black youth frees us all from the yoke of the past.

Endnotes

Excerpts from the Federal Writers' Project Slave Narrative (FWPSN) Collection

1. FWPSN, Missouri, p. 106
2. FWPSN, Mississippi, p. 155
3. FWPSN, Arkansas, Part 3, p. 180
4. FWPSN, Arkansas, Part 5, p. 351

References

DeGruy, J. A. (2005). *Post-traumatic slave syndrome: America's legacy of enduring injury and healing*. Uptone Press.

Diller, J. V. (2007). *Cultural diversity: A primer for the human services*. Brooks & Cole.

National Association of Social Workers. (2001, June 23). *NASW standards for cultural competence in social work practice*. http://www.n4a.org/datoolkit/NASW%20Standards%20II.htm

Taylor-Brown, S., Garcia, A., & Kingson, E. (2001). Cultural competence versus cultural chauvinism: Implications for social work. *Health and Social Work, 26*(3), 185–188.

■ APPENDIX A

Reflections of a Researcher

Entering the Library of Congress

Emerson et al. (1995) explains that *field notes* in ethnography are accounts describing experiences and observations the researcher has made while participating in an intense and involved manner. During the research process I experienced a wide range of emotions and thoughts, beginning with my first trip to the Library of Congress (LOC) in Washington, DC, to work with the enslaved person narratives. I knew that every narrative in the collection was available online and that I could have designed a study based on the use of the electronic medium; however, that would have provided a limited experience with the archived material. I would have lost the opportunity to review information essential to understanding the context of the Works Progress Administration (WPA) and the Federal Writers Project (FWP).

I was thrilled to receive a grant from the City University of New York's Office of Research and Sponsored Programs that covered the cost of travel to DC and lodging for an extended weekend to begin the research phase of my doctoral journey. I had done a number of things to prepare for the visit. I had read all the information on the website about procedures for the reading room of the Rare Books Division where the WPA's Federal Writers' Project Slave Narrative (FWPSN) collection was located; I had called and spoken to the assistant librarian about the collection; and I had a very detailed conversation with a member of my dissertation committee who is an expert on archival research and the LOC. What follows is my experience and observations from the first time I arrived at the majestic Madison Building of the LOC, across the street from the U.S. Capitol.

There was tight security into the building, including placing my backpack on a conveyor belt, walking through a metal detector, and being wanded for metallic weapons. The security guards were professional and purposeful. I had to secure a scholar ID card from the Reader Registration Room, and the process included presenting picture ID, then answering questions by interacting with an employee and a computer screen, and it ended with a photograph for the ID. The process lasted 15 minutes, and the scholar ID is good for 2 years. The staff person was very nice, and there was good signage throughout the building.

- I made my way to the Manuscripts Division located on the first floor/ main level and to the left from the front door.
- You must first approach the security desk and show ID.

- I received rules and regulations about appropriate behaviors, use of collection, and security.
- I signed for receipt of packet.
- I received a key to a locker to stow all my personal possessions except the laptop, chord to the laptop, and digital camera. No pencils, pens, paper, or cellphone were allowed. I signed out the key.
- I returned to the security desk and signed in the returned key.
- I was shown by security where to locate paper, pencil, copiers, and a pencil sharpener.
- Security showed me to the circulation hub, where the librarian assistants are located. My scholar ID was swiped into the system by the library assistant.
- Using a very large binder, I searched the contents of the Rare Books Division. I found what I was looking for with the help of the assistant.
- I completed an index card for the records of WPS (you can request only four at one time).
- I was assigned a table that was coded with a letter of the alphabet and a number.
- Moments later a LOC staff person delivered archived material at the table on a well-oiled cart. The materials were in folder boxes with labels on the side panel. Inside each folder box was up to four file folders. All were labeled by content and date.
- I could use a camera without a flash (so as not to damage the paper).
- There was absolutely no food or drinks permitted in the Reading Room so as not to damage the artifacts.
- Only one page of one folder from one box can be read at a time. Cardboard markers are provided as placeholders in the boxes.
- When I needed to leave the Reading Room, I had to report to security, sign out my key to my locker, get my personal items, sign in, and return the key. Then I could exit the Reading Room.
- When returning, I had to show ID, sign out the key, return all banned items to the locker, and return the key to security.
- There are security cameras everywhere. The room is extremely quiet and large. The staff was very knowledgeable and helpful. I was able to gather contextual information about the FWPSN by reading through various memorandum from the WPA field offices for the Folklore Project and from Mr. Alan Lomax, the director of the project.

The Folklore Project

I learned that the WPA-FWP developed three main projects to capture folklore of the United States, and the enslaved person narratives were the smallest part of the project, the most challenging, and the least funded. I also was able to locate the supplementary instructions to the American Guide Manual, which was the addendum to the field guide given to WPA agents who were conducting the interviews with the formerly enslaved people (see Appendix H in Milton, 2009).

The memos are carbon copies written on either hard-stock yellow paper with blue ink or on very fine, nearly transparent gray paper with black ink. Corrections were easy to spot, as many times they had pen lines across words or editing in the margins. The paper had to be handled gently and gingerly.

The Folklore Project consists of three parts: traditional folklore (music, superstitions, urban/street lore, clothing, jokes, dance), life histories (random open-ended interviews with people throughout America about who they are, what they do, where they were born, their family, etc.) and enslaved person narratives (responses to a standardized questionnaire used by field agents deployed to the South to find formerly enslaved people and document their experiences under slavery.)

The Enslaved Person Narrative Collection

After reading about the "Jersey Devil" in the traditional folklore boxes of the New Jersey collection, I turned my attention to the enslaved person narratives. The more than 2,000 narratives from 17 southern states in the collection are deposited in 33 hard-bound, green-covered books with gold lettering on the spine and edges of the pages. Each page is approximately 8.5 inches by 11 inches. The paper is hard stock, slightly yellow, and heavily odiferous from the passage of time. The volumes contain portraits of many of the contributors of the narratives and other beautiful pictures of people and places in the South. Each narrative has a unique number stamped at the top of the page, usually a six-digit number. Hand-written notes, edits in red pen, and instructions from proofreaders were evident on many pages. One needed to turn pages ever so lightly so as not to tear the paper. It was possible to reproduce copies, which was a task turned over to the librarian assistant. By the time this first session with the narratives had ended, the summer sun had set in DC, and I had seen with my very own eyes the hand-written notes of Ralph Ellison and Zora Neale Hurston and stared into the eyes in photographs of formerly enslaved people, many of whom reminded me of people in my own family, especially my grandmom. When I returned to my hotel room, exhausted from the day of research, I cried myself to sleep.

Language of the Enslaved Person Narratives

At first glance the peculiar language of this enslaved person talking about wedding do's and don'ts seems difficult to read:

> De 'oman she proud uv her nice, spankin' new broom en she lay hit on de bed fer de weddin' crowd ter see it, wid de udder things been give 'em.

> Fo' three years go by her man wuz beatin' 'er, en not long atter dat she go plum stark crazy. She oughter ter know better'n ter lay dat broom on her bed. It sho' done brung her bad luck. Dey sent her off ter de crazy folks place, en she died dar.

In more standard and modern English and grammar, this paragraph would read:

> The woman is proud of her nice, brand new broom, and she laid it on the bed for the wedding crowd to see it along side of the other things that were given to her. Three years go by, and her man was beating her and not long after that she went stark crazy. She ought to have known better than to have laid that broom on her bed. It sure did bring her bad luck. They sent her off to the crazy folks place, and she died there.

As per the supplementary instructions, the director of the Folklore Project gives explicit instructions to "write down any incident or facts he can recall as nearly as possible just as he says them but do not use dialect spelling so complicated that it may confuse the reader." I struggled very little with the dialect as recorded by the WPA agents. This is due in part to my experience with the language of enslaved people, having read literature from the genre since I was a young girl. Also, growing up in a family with a spectrum of literacy skills, I became quite accustomed to more phonetic writing and gained lots of experience in deciphering and decoding words. After immersing myself in the collection, especially during the gender indexing and the purposive sampling processes, I acquired a great deal of ease and comfort with the rhythms of the language and the storytelling of the various authors.

Immersion and Loneliness

In order to make interpretations, I needed to lose myself in the data, figure out ways to quiet my mind, and be undistracted from all the temptations of my usual life. This meant saying no to parties, family gatherings, mealtimes, theater, sitcoms, long phone calls, sports events, and a host of other pleasantries of life. In fact, the story my partner would tell friends who were inquiring about me while away on one of my research jaunts was, "Oh, Barbara isn't home; she's away with her data!" This was one of the hardest parts of the research.

There was also plenty of frustration in my many futile attempts to try to find additional collaborating information about some of the subjects in my study. Perhaps I simply lack the ability to conduct genealogical archival research at this phase of my academic life, but oh, how I would like to be mentored by the likes of Henry Louis Gates Jr. and really delve into this area of research. It isn't easy locating information for people who just didn't exist as human beings until some of the fugitive case laws were settled in the mid-19th century. Sometimes the more I immersed myself in the story, the sadder I got.

It was a lonely experience. How ironic, given the findings speak so clearly about a fundamental survival strategy for African Americans, which is to connect to others when under duress, yet here I am, doing the biggest, most stressful academic pursuit of my life, working to achieve a dream I've had since 9 years old, and in order to complete the task, to succeed, I have to disconnect from so many people I love and care about—at least until the all of the graduation celebrations begin!

Plantations and Slave Cabins

Many of the enslaved people referenced the "quarters" and "cabins." I searched online to see where in the South any remnants of these cabins were located so that I could better understand their construction, size, location on the plantation, and so on. I came upon a veritable gold mine of plantations dotting the Mississippi from New Orleans to Baton Rouge. In the summer of 2008 I decided to visit some of them. The first time I went to a plantation I booked a tour through the concierge at my hotel. I was the only African American on the bus with 15 White Midwesterners and upper Louisianians. That's a combination that unfortunately made everyone feel a little uncomfortable, particularly when we all entered the grounds of the plantation.

I had never been to a plantation. I stood on a levee on the north bank of the Mississippi River it curved toward the city of New Orleans and gazed down a long, red-earthed pathway, flanked by two parallel rows of 200-year-old hearty and robust live oaks. The magnificent trees extended from the roadway near the river to the Roman-styled, split-level mansion with a wraparound terrace. There were sprawling spiral staircases from the end of the path to the overlarge Grecco doors on the second floor of the mansion, which is the main living quarters. What I learned was that the ground floor rarely contained anything of value because the Mississippi routinely flooded, and when she did, the contents on the ground floor would be damaged.

It was a typical, sweltering summer day in the South, and I had the sweat and stickiness to prove it, but once on the path of the live oaks, it felt as if I had walked into the cool breeze of a northeastern autumn day. Amazing! I wanted to live under the trees.

A woman and man in "typical southern dress" of the 1850s met our group at the bottom of the magnificent staircase. Then we toured in the house and heard stories and gazed at objects that reflected the wealth and opulence of the family who ran the sugar plantation and "owned" the enslaved people. While in the house, the word "slavery" was not mentioned once, not even in connection with the accrual of wealth for the landowner. There were two smaller buildings that were adjacent to the main mansion. One was the kitchen and the home of the enslaved cook. Statues of "Aunt Jemima" were displayed throughout this home, along with various cast-iron pans, fine silverware, and rudimentary ovens, stoves, and ice holders. There was also a dumbwaiter system and pulley lines running from this small house into the larger house on the ground floor and then extending to the upper level. This was the system of serving food to the enslaver and his family.

The house adjacent to the main mansion was for the sons of the enslaver. When the sons entered their teen years and their years of sexual exploration, it was not uncommon for them to move out of the watchful eyes of their mothers so that they could indulge in the pastime of securing sexual trysts with enslaved girls and women.

We then walked to the back of the house and moseyed down a pathway of shrubs manicured like the English countryside that ended at another long, red-earthed pathway, with two more parallel rows of live oaks, arranged in a less dense way than those in the front of the mansion. Off to the right and left, just where the trees ended, were two parallel rows of slave cabins—22 in all. This plantation can boast that it has the largest number of preserved slave cabins in the entire South. There was a small plaque with a few words thanking the servants for their dedication to the sugar plantation and the "master". The curator of the tour showed a financial ledger to us indicating the amount of money each enslaved person cost the enslaver. Other than that factoid, nothing more was said about the enslaved people. It was time for "let's go have a mint julep" on the plantation.

I decided to go back to the same plantation the next day and met with the resident historian, who was a blood relative of the owners. While she was well versed on the family business, both when the times were exceedingly good and not so good, she held no interest in or any knowledge about the enslaved people who were once the "property" of her relatives. It was as if the enslaved people did not exist, other than on a column in a financial ledger.

After having this experience, I asked for permission to spend some time down at the enslaved person quarters to conduct some observations for my research. She thought the request was odd but granted it to me nonetheless. I spent some number of hours alone on the part of the plantation that enslaved people once roamed. I sat on the floor in the cabin, on the porch, under a live oak, alongside the sugar field. I walked to the embankment of a small lake that was thickly grown with balsawood trees. I looked up the long pathway toward the mighty Mississippi and the back of the mansion. I touched the trees. I wept. I pledged on that day to the spirit of all who were enslaved here that I would make visible their lives and their voices through my dissertation. We will never forget!

References

Emerson, R. M., Fretz, R. I. & Shaw, L. L. (1995). *Writing ethnographic fieldnotes.* Universirty of Chicago Press.

Milton, B. E., II. (2009). *"Reconnecting to resilience": A historical study of slave narratives with implications for social work practice with African American youth from high risk environments* [Doctoral dissertation]. City University of New York. CUNY Academic Works. https://academicworks.cuny.edu/gc_etds/4122

■ APPENDIX B

A Further Note on Methodology and Data Collection

Introduction

This appendix introduces the research methodology and questions that guided the qualitative inquiry to explore the enslaved person narratives for protective factors related to resilience. The best tradition of the qualitative methods that fits with the exploratory search for historical protective factors is the historical method. The unit of analysis has been defined as an individual enslaved person narrative from the FWPSN collection. The sampling procedure of the enslaved person narratives will be discussed in detail, including demographic information related to the sample. (For further explication of respondents, identification, coding process, and data analysis techniques, see Milton [2009].)

Other African American researchers have set a precedent for using qualitative methods with the narratives of formerly enslaved people to trace the genesis of cultural norms, practices, and processes and to make meaning of the lived experience of African American ancestors (Brent, 1973; Covey & Lockman, 1996; Leary, 2005; Moody, 1991; Yetman, 1970; Rawick, 1972; Taylor, 2005). This study follows that tradition. These researchers share the view that many of the pathological processes evident among African Americans today are due at least in part to being detached from their ancestral roots; and furthermore, many potentially life-sustaining and life-saving lessons may be learned in the process of reconnecting with the experience of past generations of Africans in America (Schiele, 1996).

The aim of this research was to explore through a historical lens the existence of protective factors utilized by formerly enslaved people from a sample of Federal Writers' Project slave narratives (FWPSN). The results were obtained through a three-phase process: (1) Selection of enslaved person narratives for use in the study through a sampling process of 100 narratives, which had sufficient content to be used in this study; (2) identification of excerpts from the narratives that represent an interpretation by the researcher as an example of a protective factor within an ecological domain; and (3) interpretive analysis using comparison methods to generate categories of protective factors and themes consistent across the sample of enslaved person narratives.

The Ensuing Research Questions

Data analysis yielded results to answer the following questions:

- What do the formerly enslaved people report were the individual, family, and community protective factors during slavery?
- How do the protective factors of enslaved people relate to our current understanding of the three ecological domains of human development?
- How do the historical protective factors of enslaved people compare with the protective factors for at-risk African American youth as typified by contemporary resilience research?

See the following example of an enslaved person narrative.

Alabama

de black ridge an' de twilight settle over de place spreadin' a sort of orange hue over de place. I wants to walk de paths th'ewe de woods an' see de rabbits an' watch de birds an' listen to frogs at night. But dey tuk me away f'om dat a long time ago. 'Twarn't long befo' I ma'ied an' had chilluns, but don't none of 'em 'tribute to my sppote now. One of 'em vas killed in de big var wid Germeny and de res' is all scattered out ... eight of 'em. Now I jus' live f'om han' to mouth; here one day, somewhere else de nex'. I guess we's all a-goin' to die iffen dis 'pression don't let us 'lone. Maybe someday I'll git to go home. Dey tells me dat when a pusson crosses dat ribber, de Lawd gives him whut he wants. I done tol' de Lawd I don't think dats much to axe for. I suppose he'll sen' me back dar. I been a-waitin' for hime to call.

Wash. Copy
S.L.D.
8-84-37

References

Brent, L. (1973). *Incidents in the life of a slave girl.* Harcourt Brace & Company.

Covey, H. C., & Lockman, P. T. (1996). Narrative references to older African Americans living under slavery. *The Social Science Journal, 33*(1), 23–37.

DeGruy-Leary, J. A. (2005). *Post Traumatic Slave Syndrome: America's legacy of enduring injury and healing.* Uptone Press.

Milton, B. E., II. (2009). *"Reconnecting to resilience": A historical study of slave narratives with implications for social work practice with African American youth from high risk environments* [Doctoral dissertation]. City University of New York. CUNY Academic Works. https://academicworks.cuny.edu/gc_etds/4122

Moody, J. (1991). Ripping away the veil of slavery: Literacy, communual love, and self-esteem in three women's slave narratives. *Black American Literature Forum, 24*(4), 633–648.

Rawick, G. P. (1972). *From sundown to sunup: The making of black community.* Greewood Press.

Schiele, J. H. (1996). Afrocentricity: An emerging paradigm in social work practice. Social Work, *41*(3), 284–294.

Taylor, Y. (Ed.). (2005). *Growing up in slavery: Stories of young slaves as told by themselves.* Lawrence Hill Books.

Yetman, N. R. (1970). *Voices from slavery.* Dover Publications, Inc.

The Federal Writers' Project, Selection from "Alabama Narratives," *Slave Narratives: A Folk History of Slavery in the United States*, p. 110. 1941.

APPENDIX C

Names of Formerly Enslaved People Whose Wisdom Is Captured in This Book

John Barker: Texas
Fannie Berry: Virginia
Maggie Black: South Carolina
Rias Body: Georgia
Dan Bogie: Kentucky
James Bolton: Georgia
Phoebe Bost: Ohio
Bernice Bowden: Arkansas
Jerry Boykins: Texas
Joseph William Carter: Indiana
Susan Castle: Georgia
Wiley Childress: Tennessee
Maria Sutton Clements: Arkansas
Mary Divine: Missouri
Doc Daniel Dowdy: Oklahoma
Washington Dozier: South Carolina
Delia Garlic: Alabama
James Goings: Missouri
Rachal Goings: Missouri
Fannie Griffin: South Carolina
Della Harris: Virginia
Rachel Harris: Arkansas
Tom Hawkins: Georgia
Bill Heard: Georgia
George Henderson: Kentucky
Annie Young Henson: Maryland
Clayton Holbert: Kansas
Eliza Ison: Kentucky
Camilla Jackson: Georgia
George Jackson: Ohio
Martin Jackson: Texas
Nancy Jackson: Texas
Rev. Squires Jackson: Florida
Marion Johnson: Arkansas
Samuel Johnson: Florida
Bob Jones: North Carolina
Ellis Ken Kannon: Tennessee
Jennie Kendricks: Georgia
James Lucas: Mississippi
Susan Matthews: Georgia
Bert Mayfield: Kentucky
Lucy McCullough: Georgia
Anna Miller: Texas
Gracie Mitchell: Arkansas
America Morgan: Indiana
Clairborne Moss: Arkansas
Horace Overstreet: Texas
Sarah Pittman: Arkansas
Laura Ramsey Parker: Tennessee
Delicia Lucinda Patterson: Missouri
Frank Range: South Carolina
Irene Robertson: Arkansas
Rosaline Rogers: Indiana
Alexander Scaife: South Carolina
Willie Ann Smith: Texas
Isaac Stier: Mississippi

Jane Sutton: Mississippi
Maria Sutton Clemments: Arkansas
Anthony Taylor: Arkansas
Jim Taylor: Maryland
Warren Taylor: Arkansas
Lucindia Washington: Alabama
Dianah Watson: Texas
Belle Williams: Kansas
Willis Williams: Florida
Eliza Williamson: Georgia
Uncle Willis: Georgia
Mary Jane Wilson: Virginia
Maggie Woods: Arkansas
Henry Wright: Georgia

Index

A

adolescent
- African Americans, 35
- brain development, 38

adults parentifying kids, 60
advocacy
- at meso level, 102
- direct individual, 102–103
- legislative and campaign, 103–104

affirmation of individual worth, 22–34
afraid, 39–40
after-school program, 113
- child, 53

Amendment to the Constitution (14th), 10–11
Americans With Disabilities Act, 10
assault
- of White supremacy, 1
- on individual agency, 17–22
- on individual Black body, 17–22
- sexual, 110

B

Barker, J., 84
basic needs, 49–50, 61, 92
Bell, D., 3
benevolence, 94–96
Black Americans, 2
- experience of oppression, 5
- familial connections for, 58–60
- lag behind European Americans, 3
- personal and collective resistance, 4

Black community, 85–87
- need of White investment, 87

Black girl with bipolar disorder, 19–22
Black girl with low self-esteem, 24–25
Black Lives Matter, 9, 88, 97
Black, M., 25
Black young female, 30–31, 33, 54–55, 57, 73–74
Black young male, 27–29, 31–34, 49–50, 52, 57–58
Black youth, 40
- connecting to Black elders, 86
- connecting to leaders, 85
- leadership to, 85
- LGBTQIA+, 87–88
- mentoring of, 86
- safety of, 103–104
- supporting entrepreneurship, 86

Blow, C. M., 108
Body, R., 26
Bogie, D., 49, 71
Bolton, J., 26, 69, 70, 92, 94–95, 96
Bost, P., 25
Boulton, J., 57
Bowden, B., 30, 32
Boykins, J., 26, 92
brain science, 38
Bronfenbrenner, U., 4
brown-skinned young student, 55–56
Brown v. Board of Education, 11

C

Cahill, H., 5
Cannon, F., 9
care, defined, 48–51
Carter, J. W., 32
Castle, S., 25
CETA program (Comprehensive and Employment Training Act), 93
chattel slavery, 2
childhood, 112
Childress, W., 53
Clemments, M. S., 26, 29, 98
clinical settings, 115–117
- foundation for practice in, 37–38

Coates, T.-N., 107
code switching
- community, 67–68

communication, strengthening of, 61

community, 65–87
Black community, 85–87
code switching, 67–68
double consciousness, 67–68
implications, 82–85
personal experience with, 69–70
protective factors, 68–82
competence of, 25–29
Cooper, B., 108
corrective to erasure, 22–34
counsel, defined, 51–53
critical race theory (CRT), 3–4, 114
cultural groups, 61–62
cultural heritage, 75–79
cultural humility, 115

D

data collection, 125–126
DeGruy, J., 85, 107, 112
direct individual advocacy, 102–103
Divine, M., 29, 116
double consciousness/dual consciousness, 67–68
personal stories, 83–85
Dowdy, D. D., 71
Dozier, W., 29
Du Bois, W.E.B., 67

E

Earhart, A., 7
EdBuild, 10
education, 115–117
foundation for practice in, 37–38
public funding, 10
educators/teachers, 8
implications for, 10–12, 34–36, 58–60, 114–117
Sankofa guidelines for, 38–41, 85–87, 100–102
electoral activism, 9
Ellison, R., 121
enslaved people, 127–128
affirmation of individual worth, 22–34
aid of, 92–94
competence of, 25–29
passion, 32–34
personal power, 23–25
spirituality, 29–32
enslavement, 107–117
chattel, 12
conversation with Black community, 109–113
implications for professional social workers and educators, 114–117
parents, 53
protective factors, 114
residuals, 3
White community, 113–114
enslavers, 18, 24, 36, 47, 65–66, 104

F

familial connection (family domain), 12
family, 45–62
dynamics, 61
familial connections for Black Americans, 58–60
intervention, 8
outside of, 60
protective factors, 47–58
working with, 60–62
Federal Writers' Project (FWP), 116, 119
Federal Writers' Project slave narratives (FWPSN), 125
Floyd, G., 97
Folklore Project, 120–121
From Sundown to Sunup (Rawick), 22

G

Garlic, D., 30, 53
Goings, J., 32
Goings, R., 26
goods and services, 92–94
Gorman, A., 108
Griffin, F., 79

H

Harris, D., 23, 29
Harris, R., 23, 117
Hawkins, T., 71, 79
Heard, B., 30, 51, 54, 68
Henderson, G., 97
Henson, A. Y., 24
Holbert, C., 68, 69
Hoyle, P., 73
Hughes, L., 107
Hurricane Sandy, 70
Hurston, Z. N., 121

I

immersion and loneliness, 122–123
implications
community, 83–86
for educators, 10–12, 34–36, 58–60, 114–117

for social workers, 6–10, 34–36, 58–60, 114–117
individual agency, 17–22
individual Black body, 17–22
in-group connection (the enslaved community), 12
intergenerational trauma, 60
internal connection (individual domain), 12, 34–36
Ison, E., 94

J

Jackson, C., 24, 29, 56, 71, 73–74
Jackson, G., 27, 48
Jackson, M., 32, 51
Jackson, N., 69
Jackson, S., 25, 27–29, 80, 81
Jim Crow, 1, 3, 18
Johnson, M., 30, 49
Johnson, S., 33
Jones, E. P., 104

K

Kannon, E. K., 26
Kendricks, J., 24, 29, 51
King, M. L. Jr., 7, 12
Klu Klux Klan, 97
Kolchin, P., 47
Ku Klux Klan, 23, 38

L

Latinos, 6
Latinx, 18, 37, 115
LGBTQIA+ Black youth, 87–88
Library of Congress (LOC), 119–120
Logsdon, A., 11
loneliness and immersion, 122–123
Loyed, M., 93
Lucas, J., 54, 79

M

Mandela, N., 38
Martin, T., 82–83
Matthews, S., 48
Mayfield, B., 79, 98
Mccullough, L., 25, 79
Meckler, L., 10
microaggressions, 38–39
Miller, A., 92, 93
Millie, A., 85
Mitchell, G., 48
models, defined, 53–56
Morgan, A., 98
movement for Black lives (M4BL), 4
Murray, P., 108
mutual support, defined, 68–70

N

National Association of Social Workers (NASW), 4
norms
    and values, 81–82
    defined, 79–83
    personal experience with, 80

O

Obama, B., 9
Obama, M., 108
opportunity
    defined, 71–74, 98–100
    personal experience with, 71–73
out-group connection, 12
    macro, micro and mezzo levels, 102–104
    protective factors, 92–100
    white allies and officials, 100–102
Overstreet, H., 56

P

Parker, L. R., 92
Parks, R., 7
passion, 32–34
Patrick, K., 11
Patterson, D., 68
Patterson, L., 24, 39
personal experience, 93–94
    with community, 69–70
    with norms, 80
    with opportunity, 71–73
personal power, 23–25
person's fight to overcome, 2–6
Pittman, S., 117
plantations and slave cabins, 123–124
post-traumatic slave syndrome (PTSS), 116
practitioners, 8
    practitioners
    Sankofa guidelines for, 85–87
    Sankofa guidelines for, 38–41, 85–87, 100–102
pride, defined, 75–79
protection, defined, 96–98
protective factors
    community, 68–82
    family domain, 47–58
    out-group connection, 92–100
Pryor, R., 111

R

Rawick, G., 22, 67
Reagon, B. J., 85
relationships with people, 61–62
religious institutions, 29–32
research methodology, 125–126
research questions, 126
resilience
  defined, 4
  historical trauma, 2–6
  in education, 5
  person's fight to overcome, 2–6
Rice, T., 40
rituals, defined, 56–58
Robertson, I., 93, 98
Rogers, R., 53
Rogers, S., 29
Roosevelt, T., 7
Ross, B., 7

S

Sankofa guidelines, 7
  for educators, 38–41, 85–87, 100–102
  for practitioners, 38–41, 85–87, 100–102
Scaife, A., 26, 79
selective hearing, 34
slave cabins and plantations, 123–124
slave narratives
  collection, 121
  language of, 121–122
slave patrols, 18
Smiley, T., 11
social workers, 6–10, 34–36, 114–117
spirituality, 29–32
Stier, I., 52, 99
Stowers, S., 99
supporting children in their activities, 61
Sutton, J., 29, 56
systemic racism, 1, 88, 93

T

Taylor, A., 30, 57, 96–97
Taylor, J., 68
Taylor, W., 51
The Covenant (Smiley), 11
The Known World (Jones), 104
The New York Times, 110
toughness, 39
trauma
  historical, 2–6
  intergenerational, 60
Tubman, H., 38

V

values and norms, 81–82

W

Washington, G., 7
Washington, L., 29, 30, 97
Watson, D., 29, 30, 94
We are human, 108
White allies and officials, 100–102
Williams, B., 25
Williamson, E., 94
Williams, R., 111
Williams, W., 48, 49, 51, 94
Willis, U., 30
Wilson, M. J., 94, 95
Withers, B., 73
Woods, M., 81, 84
work for justice, 85
Wright, D., 31
Wright, H., 48, 69, 80, 98

Y

young Black student, 18–19

About the Authors

Image 1.0: Copyright © by Reena Rose Sibayan/Jersey Journal. Reprinted with permission.

Barbara Ella Milton Jr., PhD, LCSW, a clinical social worker, clinical supervisor, social work educator, child welfare advocate, activist, social media producer, author, and resilience expert, has been an impactful social change agent for the wellness of at-risk youth and families for decades. She is a contributor to the *Confessions of a Welfare Mom* series and coauthor of *The Great Pause: Blessings and Wisdom from COVID-19* book and journal, as well as an opinion in the journal *Psychosis*. She is the author of *Heeding the Caregiver Call: The Story of Barbara Ella Milton, Sr. and Alzheimer's Disease*. Dr. Milton is currently working on another manuscript titled *The Versatility of the Social Work Profession*. She wrote a column for the *Jersey Journal* that put a spotlight on resilient teens called Our Pride and Joy and now enjoys regular submissions of op-ed essays on social issues. She produced and hosted a television show on Public Access/Comcast called *Dr. Milton's Social Work Show* to educate the community at large about the social work profession and social welfare issues. Dr. Milton was an adjunct professor at several schools of social work in New Jersey and New York City. She is the past chair of the National Association of Social Workers (NASW), NJ Chapter, Hudson County Unit and the New Jersey Chapter of NASW's 2014 Social Worker of the Year. Dr. Milton was born in Camden, New Jersey, as the only child of Barbara Ella Milton Sr., who died from Alzheimer's in January 2019. She lives in North Jersey with her wife, Kay. They enjoy a life rich with family and friends. Please follow Dr. Milton's life and work at www.DrBarbaraEMiltonJrLCSW.com.

Image 1.1

Deborah Brooks Lawrence, EdD, is a native New Yorker who believes that equitable access to viable resources will pave the road for universal recognition and sustainability of human rights and that, as educators, we, without question, need to prepare all of our practitioners and students to embrace the possibilities of equitable opportunity. This is couched in her witness to, and participation in, the civil rights and women's movements as well as her firsthand witness to apartheid and Nyerere's Pan-Africanism. It is through this inclusive lens that she weaves theory, research, advocacy, and practice in her current role as a child welfare specialist and contract manager with the City of New York. Alongside her current role, Dr. Lawrence created and taught an integrated course on the foundations of education for Bank Street College of Education, was a teaching fellow and part of the teaching team in educational leadership and development for the Summer Principal's Academy (SPA) at Columbia University, and, most recently, co-taught a dissertation research course at Teacher's College Columbia University. Prior to this work, she taught logic and rhetoric for Antioch College's NY Extension, taught in a charter elementary school, and was the founding director of the only supplemental educational program to mandate parents' attendance to learn and discover alongside their children. Dr. Lawrence's scope of work includes work as the interim director with ReServe (an organization for retired individuals), education director of in-school, out-of-school, and after-school programs throughout NYC for a large nonprofit, work on tolerance with the United Nations Association of the United States of America (UNA-USA), and pivotal work with immigrant populations, disenfranchised adults, marginalized children and families, and education and child welfare practitioners.